"I've been blessed to see how Julie's teaching can unhitch a church and family from the crazy train. And I'm so thankful that many more will be challenged and encouraged by this wonderful book." —Collin Hansen, editorial director of The Gospel Coalition and author of *Blind Spots: Becoming a Courageous, Compassionate, and Commissioned Church*

"In *Unhitching from the Crazy Train*, Julie Sparkman invites us to experience a meal of pure gospel with a garnishing of beautiful humor that causes us to lean in and laugh. The result is that we experience more of our Savior in everyday life and learn how to trust Him for the rest He promises as we walk with Him. We have been immeasurably blessed by Julie's teaching and have shared it with hundreds of others who have used it to unhitch from an orphan mentality and live in the freedom of belief." —Susan and Newt Crenshaw, president of Young Life

"*Unhitching from the Crazy Train* is an enlightening, encouraging resource for examining what we rely on and helping us place our trust in Christ. This book has helped me and many I know to jump off that crazy train . . . or to never hop on in the first place!" —Lauren Hansen, deacon of women's ministry, Redeemer Community Church, Birmingham, AL

"*Unhitching from the Crazy Train* is a book about being, not doing. It is an invitation to embrace the gospel in a lived out kind of way rather than simply a talked about kind of way. It is written in a conversational manner, but there is such depth to every single sentence. By prayerfully and practically engaging in this book you can become more grace-filled and gospel-centered through the refinement of your soul in Jesus Christ." —Kristen Torres, minister of spiritual development, Dawson Memorial Baptist Church, Birmingham, AL

"If you're clinging to the crazy train, determined that your performance as a parent, a spouse, or a Christian is going to get you to the good life, this wise book is an invitation to disembark. Chapter by chapter, you'll inhale the sweet aroma of an ancient invitation, 'Come unto me, all ye that labor and are heavy laden, and I will give you rest' (Matthew 11:28)."—Ray Cortese, pastor, Seven Rivers Presbyterian Church, Lacanto, FL

"*Unhitching from the Crazy Train* is for those looking for a deeper walk with Jesus and longing to invite Him into the broken places of your life. It is for those who are at a place where you realize grace won't fix you in this life but is simply the power of Christ that enables broken people with broken lives in this broken world to experience substantial healing and progress. Honest, authentic, at times even raw, this book is biblical, grace-centered, and filled with hope in Christ . . . for you and for me." —Bob Flayhart, founding and senior pastor, Oak Mountain Presbyterian Church, Birmingham, AL

"The teaching and studies by Julie Sparkman have been a blessing to the women of our church and are a staple of our women's Bible study curriculum. It was a delight to read *Unhitching from the Crazy Train* now in book form! This book provides biblical truths, insights, and tools that help guide our thinking as we learn to come to Jesus, resting in Him." —Karen Pourcho, director of women's ministry, College Park Church, Indianapolis, IN

"Jennifer and Julie understand and communicate clearly how the gospel is utterly practical, not just for our eternal salvation but for the daily sanctification that takes place in our messy kitchens, the aisles of Walmart, and bumper-to-bumper traffic. This teaching will challenge, inspire, convict, and encourage readers. I am certain God will use this book to teach believers how to hear, follow, and find rest in Jesus above the roar of the crazy train." —Anna Meade Harris, Rooted blog parent editor, preministerial scholars coordinator at Samford University (Birmingham, AL), and author of *Fresh Faith: Topical Devotions and Scripture-Based Prayers for College Students*

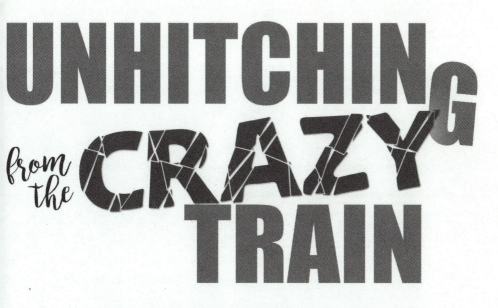

UNHITCHING
from the CRAZY TRAIN

Finding Rest in a World You Can't Control

JULIE SPARKMAN
WITH JENNIFER PHILLIPS

NEW HOPE®
PUBLISHERS

BIRMINGHAM, ALABAMA

New Hope® Publishers
5184 Caldwell Mill Rd
St. 204-221
Hoover, AL 35244
NewHopePublishers.com
New Hope Publishers is a division of Iron Stream Media.

Library of Congress Cataloging-in-Publication Data

Names: Sparkman, Julie, author.
Title: Unhitching from the crazy train : finding rest in a world you can't
   control / Julie Sparkman with Jennifer Phillips.
Description: First [edition]. | Birmingham : New Hope Publishers, 2017.
Identifiers: LCCN 2017036548 | ISBN 9781625915368 (permabind)
Subjects: LCSH: Rest--Religious aspects--Christianity. | Providence and
   government of God--Christianity. | Stress management--Religious
   aspects--Christianity. | Christian women--Religious life.
Classification: LCC BV4597.55 .S63 2017 | DDC 248.4--dc23
LC record available at https://lccn.loc.gov/2017036548

ISBN-13: 978-1-62591-536-8

N184109 • 0118 • 1M2

DEDICATION

To my family

Wes, Brent, Allie, Julianne, Anna Claire, and Carter

No matter how many trips I've taken on the Crazy Train, you were always waiting for me when I got back.

And to Sally

whose faithful and loving pursuit of my heart showed me the power of the gospel in the context of relationship.

I am forever grateful.

CONTENTS

ACKNOWLEDGMENTS

From *Julie*

The book you now hold is a testimony to the truth that "we are God's handiwork, created in Christ Jesus to do good works, which God prepared in advance for us to do" (Ephesians 2:10). I have been asked for years if I would ever consider writing a book, and my response has always been the same: "I would rather give birth to a fourth child." You can never be sure of the good works that God has for you, but He is indeed faithfully preparing you long before it is time to walk in them.

God prepared me by giving me the honor of hearing my clients' stories as we journeyed together toward healing and restoration.

He prepared me with the teaching of pastors, teachers, and incredibly dear, gracious friends who faithfully modeled the truths of the gospel and loved me well.

He prepared me by blessing me with a husband and children who have unwittingly been my greatest learning lab for life and relationships. They've had the courage to be authentic in their love for me and offered forgiveness for my many failures.

And He prepared me by providing a fellow traveler in Jennifer Phillips, a woman who truly lives what she writes. She is as funny as she is deep. Her talent made this project possible, but her heart made the journey a joy.

We were made for good works that we may not see coming but are prepared for nonetheless because He never calls us to something for which He does not equip us. We need not fear; we can anticipate with hope what lies ahead. And we can rest.

From *Jennifer*

I am so grateful to my family for enduring the absurdity of me writing my third book in three years. You have endured my "expressions of stress," aka, going full on mean mama, when I felt the pressure of this project. Thank you for forgiving me and loving me when I was at my worst. Thank you for encouraging me and cheering me on, even going so far as to fill out prayer cards at church on my behalf. I love you. I pray we will each rest in Jesus a little more every day.

Thank you to all my dear friends who cheered me on during this project, who told me countless times to keep going when I wanted to quit, and who babysat Lucy so I could have extra time to write. I love you all, and I am forever indebted to your thoughtfulness, kindness, and generosity.

Thank you, thank you, thank you, Julie Sparkman, for giving me such an incredible opportunity—for trusting me with your thoughts and your words. Thank you for counseling me from the pages of this book and from the other side of the world during our weekly phone catch-ups. It has been such an honor to watch you live out what you teach as we stumbled through this ridiculously hard task of book writing. Thank you for showering me with grace upon grace, for repeatedly pointing me to Jesus, and for making me laugh when we were both at our absolute wit's end. Thank you for not firing me when I tried to sneak in phrases like "skillz" and "mic drop." We may write that next book yet: *The Writing of Unhitching from the Crazy Train: The Untold Story.* Love you, friend.

Most of all, thank You, Jesus. To You be all the glory for every word in this book. May You use the words on these pages to draw eyes and hearts to Yourself.

PREFACE

By *Jennifer Phillips*

When I was ten years old, I found out my hero—the great Larnelle Harris—was going to do a concert at our church. I loved Larnelle. His music stirred my young, little soul. I often cried real tears when I listened to his ballad, "I Miss My Time with You," and he brought a good old-fashioned gospel revival to my heart every time I heard him sing "Amen." So when I heard he was coming to town, my first thought was obviously, *When will I get my phone call from Larnelle asking me to sing Sandi Patty's part in "I've Just Seen Jesus"?* Surely he would ask me. I may have only been in fifth grade, but I thought, *Our music minister has heard me sing. I'm sure he'll pass on my name and number. It's only a matter of time.*

I am not exaggerating. I really thought he would call. Or, you know, one of his people would call. I had to wait 28 long years to get a phone call from my hero but it was no longer Larnelle; it was Julie Sparkman.

A friend introduced me to some material from Julie's study, *Idol Addiction*, when I was in the middle of an immigration crisis with my adopted little girl. I was so encouraged by the truth in her words that I did the full study twice with women in my church and then followed it up with another one of her lecture series, *Unhitching from the Crazy Train*. To say I was a Julie fan was an understatement. I had never heard the gospel so clearly explained; I had never felt my heart so exposed, yet so loved and free, as when I listened to those two studies. I quoted her all the time and used her flow charts on my kids, because what child does not want his emotions and behaviors plotted on a whiteboard at the dinner table? Needless to say, God was using the gospel truths in Julie's material to radically change my family and my relationships.

Imagine my surprise when I awoke one morning to an email from Julie herself. She began with these words: "When I read what you write, I feel like you write the way I would write if I could write."

Pardon me? She reads what I write? At the time, I had published one book, *Bringing Lucy Home*, and had only been blogging consistently for a few years. *She reads my stuff??* Stop the press. Julie went on:

"I would like to turn my lecture series, *Unhitching from the Crazy Train*, into a book. Would you be interested in doing that with me?"

Would I be interested in doing that with her? *Are you kidding me?* I was ten years old again, and the great Larnelle had called and invited me to join him on stage. I couldn't believe it. We got to work right away on a book proposal and were thrilled when it was quickly approved. I jumped straight into the manuscript full throttle. Julie had entrusted her work to me, and you'd better believe I was going to make her proud. I wrote and I wrote and I wrote, fingers flying across the keyboard, convinced my words would be the answer to Julie's prayers. She was going to be so thankful for me. So proud of me. I just knew it.

What do you get when you take someone whose intangible idols are approval and success and throw them into a writing project with their living, breathing idol, whose work has changed their life? The perfect storm of insecurity.

You are going to read a lot in this book about pictures—pictures of how you want life to be, of how you look to people and circumstances to fulfill you. I had a picture, all right. I had a picture of me writing the most stunning adaptation of *Unhitching from the Crazy Train*, sending it to Julie chapter by chapter, and her responding with all caps and exclamation points, "THIS IS AMAZ-ING!!!!!!!!!!!!!!!!!!!!!! YOU ARE AMAZING!!!!!!!!!!!!!!!!!!!!!!!"

That's not quite what happened. Instead, I sent her content I thought was Pulitzer-Prize worthy, and she wasn't sure about it. She had questions. She wanted parts written again.

Say what?

You need to know that I am a wee bit of an overachiever. In high school, it wasn't enough to get an A; I had to get 100 per-cent—and really, higher than 100 percent, what with honors classes being weighted and all. My standard for myself (when it comes to things I believe I'm good at, not things like baking or Pinterest crafts) is to knock it out of the park the very first time. There is no room for error. My expectation is that I will do a bang-up job, and I will then accept my trophy, thank you very much. So when one of the people I respect the most—the one whose teaching had lit-erally transformed the way I think about my relationship with God and others, the one I desperately wanted to please—didn't think I nailed it on the first try, I was devastated.

What? Does this mean no trophy?

As I was writing a book about unhitching from the crazy train, I was hitching myself to Julie's approval with every chapter sent and every email and phone call I received in return. Even though my messages were peppy and confident—"Here's chapter 4! Woo hoo! Let me know what you think!"—between the lines I was pleading, "Please tell me you love it. Please. Please validate my worth with your response."

I have never felt as exposed as I felt while working on this project. Every fear, every insecurity, was forced to the surface with nowhere to hide. In a case of life imitating art, I realized my emo-tional stability was tied to Julie's stamp of approval. As I typed about how we are suffocated by our efforts to get life from sources other than Christ, I was confronted with how I had been drinking from the broken cistern of the applause of people. As I described the freedom offered in the gospel, I pled, "Jesus, free me! I don't want to be a slave anymore to my pictures of approval and praise." As I wrote truths of God's provision and righteousness, I said, "Yes, Lord. That's right. My righteousness does not rest in my success. I have nothing to prove. You are enough."

This book was not written from a place of self-sufficiency, as in, "Here's what you needy people need to know about how to do this Christian thing well." It was written from a place of desperation, my idols staring me square in the face, asking, "Who are you going to worship?" As I sat under Julie's teaching once again, this time as coauthor, I begged God to give me the courage to walk away from those broken cisterns and allow His freedom, stability, and rest to breathe life into my anxious soul.

Writing this book with Julie has been one of the greatest privileges of my life but not for the reasons I first thought. What started out as an ego boost because my hero thought I was a good enough writer to entrust me with her material turned into a yearlong process of false gods being revealed and stripped away. Every chapter was an opportunity for God to ask me again, "Where do you place your hope, Jennifer? Is it in My righteousness or your reputation? Are you going to rest in Me?" By walking through these questions with Julie by my side, as my friend, I learned more about God's tender grace and precious provision than I could have ever anticipated.

We got there in the end. As Julie and I persevered through honesty, with a commitment to calling out the best in each other while wrapped in the safety of the gospel, a synergy emerged, producing a quality of material better than either of us could have done on our own. We experienced firsthand that when you are free from the burdens of expectations and approval, you're free to be the very best version of yourself—who you were created to be, doing what you were created to do.

As you read these chapters and wade into the scary waters of vulnerability, know that both authors waded through them to write it. Have courage, dear friend. Your Savior holds your hand, and His eyes are kind. I pray the refinement and freedom I experienced in the writing process will be your story as you engage with Christ's tender, costly invitation throughout these pages: "Come."

INTRODUCTION

What This Book Is Not

I have a confession to make. I'm afraid the title of this book has misled you, and you're going to resent me for it.

It's an understandable mistake. If I were you and did not know me, I could easily pick up a book called *Unhitching from the Crazy Train*, hear the angels sing as heavenly light glistens off the cover, and shout, "Eureka! I've found it! Here lie the answers I've been looking for! I might as well be a conductor on the crazy train, and this woman is going to help me get off by telling me how to organize my chaotic life. Praise the Lord! I'll take 18 copies, please."

Oh, dear.

If you knew me at all, you would know that I am neither organized nor efficient, so I can't really help you make behavior charts or color-coded calendars. If you bought this book with the hope that I would turn you into a better version of yourself by the end of eight chapters, you might want to return it. I hope you don't.

Honestly, even if I did have great organizational skills, I wouldn't write a book about them. Enough people have written those kinds of books and written them well. No, I wouldn't write a book about how to achieve a life balance so that you can do better, feel better, or act better because I don't think the chaos of life is actually what is making you crazy. I think the problem goes deeper than that.

The truth is, you had a picture in your mind of how you thought life would turn out. This picture is made up of lots of components—your job, your marriage, your children—everything you hope life to be, including your own performance. Sometimes life matches your picture. But more often than not, reality does not match what you hope it to be. So, you work harder; you strategize, demand, and control, frantically grasping at the wind in order to achieve your picture, and you are exhausted.

You are officially hitched to the crazy train. Your mood and outlook are connected to the picture in your head. When life closely resembles your picture, you feel happy and energized. But when reality veers away from that desired picture, it carries your emotional, spiritual, and sometimes even your physical stability along with it. You become preoccupied with corralling everyone and everything into your picture of how things *should* be.

What makes this response crazy is the fact that even as you are engaging in these exhausting efforts, you know they are futile. Think of the speed and size of an actual train. Would you ever try to stop a train with your bare hands? Would you attempt to corral it onto a different track? Of course not. In the same way, we cannot force people and circumstances into our desired picture. But we keep trying, don't we? And that's just plain crazy.

We may not be able to make life and people cooperate so that our picture comes true, but we can choose not to hitch to our picture. We can remain stable and grounded even while we are profoundly disappointed.

More than a self-help plan, this book is an invitation to unhitch from the crazy train. As Christians, we are called to a way of life characterized by sanity, stability, and rest, even though life may not have turned out how we pictured it to be. This invitation will sometimes feel painful. We will peer into some vulnerable places, touching wounds that are still raw with disappointment. Your true theology might be revealed, the one you really live by, and it may be different from the one you talk about on Sunday mornings or try to teach your children. You may discover that although you say you know the truth, it has not set you free in the day-to-day challenges of life. Facing this gap between what you know and how you live is essential if you are ever going to understand why you continue to be emotionally controlled by people and circumstances rather than resting in what Christ has done for you.

Don't be afraid of what the Spirit may reveal; your Father knows you, loves you, and is for you.

As these tender places of your heart are exposed, keep in mind that the transformation you long for is no more your responsibility than your God-given righteousness is. You did not save yourself, and apart from the Spirit's work, you are incapable of changing yourself. You can, however, choose to present your heart and mind before God, asking Him to reveal your unbelief, remind you of what is true, and align your heart with His Word. Don't be afraid of what the Spirit may reveal; your Father knows you, loves you, and is for you.

Think of yourself as the buyer of a house. When we were selling our first home, the worst part of the process was inspection day. I cleaned, patched, and painted any possible defect that the inspector might look at a little too closely. I feared the exposure of costly repairs we would be responsible to fix, lest we lose our contract. When the inspector arrived, I was sweating bullets. The only feedback I wanted to hear was, "Well, haven't you decorated this place nicely? I'm sure this won't take me long at all. I'll breeze on through and then be on my way."

When the buyer arrived, his perspective was completely different. He approached inspection day with a keen interest in everything the inspector discovered. He wanted to hear everything the inspector had to say. "What are you looking at over there? Can I see too? What do you think needs to be done?"

What is the difference between me as the seller and the buyer of my home? Why was I afraid and the buyer curious? Because I knew that whatever was exposed, I was responsible to fix; I would have to come up with the resources to make it right. On the other hand, the buyer wanted everything exposed because he wanted to move into a fully functioning home, and he knew someone else was responsible for the money and labor required to make that happen. He knew that even though the repairs might cause a mess in the meantime, the end result would be worth it.

As we journey together to uncover the areas of unbelief in your life, the places where you are trusting in your picture of how life should be instead of in Jesus, I want you to see yourself as the buyer. No matter what is exposed in your soul by the Holy Spirit, God already knows about it. He knows all about your secret vulnerabilities, and He has already begun the process of transformation—a soul renovation that has been paid in full. Allow yourself to be curious in anticipation of what He is up to.

You may feel skeptical right now. You may be thinking, *How can one book evoke this kind of change? You have no idea the things I've already tried, and they just haven't worked.* It's a tall order, I know. Truthfully, change will not happen as you simply read these chapters. Insight? Yes. But insight, in and of itself, does not lead to change. Insight combined with the Spirit, however, leads to repentance, and repentance leads to lasting change.

I have a couple of tips to help get this material from your head to your heart. First of all, process the ideas I share in this book with someone else you love and trust. Learning rarely happens apart from community, so talk to someone about what God is teaching you through the truths in these pages. Tell that person how to pray for you as you are confronted with the parts of yourself you'd rather not see; ask that friend to encourage you as you're asked to surrender control and you feel vulnerable and exposed. Enlist friends to pray protection over whatever God is seeking to do in your life so that you don't become distracted, discouraged, or confused.

Second, complete the process questions at the end of each chapter. I often tell my clients that the majority of the work of transformation is not done in my office. In each counseling session, I essentially pack a backpack for them and then instruct them to go home, dump out the backpack, and process with God whatever they heard during our time together. In the same way, it's important for you to know that the words within these pages are not the answer. I am not the answer giver. I am merely a small conduit that God is using to access and change your heart. The process questions are essential. *Do not skip the process questions* because that's where the real work will happen between you and the Lord.

There is much work to do. It is work to get before God and hear Him. It can be relatively easy to do a Bible study; it is work to engage God.

The posture with which you approach the process questions is critical. It is crucial you come to the Father with a heart that is ready to receive. Your job is to show up, eager to learn; His job is to change your heart.

My prayer is that when you reach the end of this book, you will be disrupted. Scary word, I know, but hang in there. When we arrive at points in our lives, big or small, when our reality does not match the picture we had hoped for, it is a true coming of age in our faith. Our response to disappointment provides a window into our soul, and we must be brave enough to peer through the glass. We honor God when we engage Him in our pain and confusion.

Ask Him the questions you thought you never should. In raw honesty, process with Him what you discover. If you don't understand aspects of the message in this book, ask Him to make them clear for you. Trust in Jesus, who will give you eyes to see, but do the work to position yourself to understand.

My aim is not to give you more information but to help you use what you may already know. As a counselor in the Bible Belt, I see many Christians who have been in church for decades. They know how to share the gospel, yet they do not know how to apply that same gospel to their everyday lives. They remain enslaved to the burden of attempting to make life work by trying harder. I'm afraid freedom is scarce in the evangelical world today. *Don't let this be the case with you.* Don't settle for knowing the lingo of the family but never really feeling a part. Press in; be honest before the Father. Ask Him for what you most deeply desire: freedom that can only come from Him.

The journey to freedom is a slow one, I'm afraid. The truths you must embrace to get there are more like an antibiotic than a steroid shot. A steroid shot is fast acting. You feel its effects almost immediately after you take it. We want the gospel to be this way, don't we? We want to meditate on it and instantly feel better. Sometimes that happens, but more often than not, the gospel works like an antibiotic. An antibiotic is taken in faith because you don't feel well right away; it takes a few days. But you keep taking it because you trust the doctor who said the medicine is healing you, even though you cannot see or feel progress.

Trust the Great Physician who says, "If you are in My Word, if you are seeking My face, change is happening inside your heart. I promise. Keep meeting with Me, keep listening to Me, and eventually, you'll see transformation." John 14:26 says, "But the Advocate, the Holy Spirit, whom the Father will send in my name, will teach

you all things and will remind you of everything I have said to you."
What a relief! Jesus will teach you, and the Spirit will remind you of
what He has taught. Accept these promises by faith.

If you stick with me these next eight chapters, you won't get
your ten-step plan toward a better you. You won't walk away with
a new life-management system. You will be disrupted and flipped
upside-down. You may feel more disheveled than ever. But you
could, perhaps, embrace sweet freedom for the very first time. You
might possibly experience the gospel breathing new life into your
weary soul.

Come to me, all you who are weary
and burdened, and I will give you rest.
Take my yoke upon you and learn from me,
for I am gentle and humble in heart,
and you will find rest for your souls.

—Matthew 11:28–29

Chapter 1

Are You Done Yet?

I entered the waiting room of our counseling offices to greet my new clients, Joe and Jill. As she stood, Jill lifted a full-length, framed photo of her family. I couldn't help but notice how happy the family in the photo looked. From the picture smiled three good-looking kids, arms around each other, along with their very much still-in-love mom and dad, all standing together in front of a lovely home. Joe brought along an equally large framed image. His portrait included himself surrounded by his adoring family and proud work colleagues who were all beaming at him as he accepted a fancy plaque bearing the words, "Atta boy, Joe."

Though it was a tight fit, we all managed to cram into my counseling room. I began our session as I usually do.

"So, how can I help you?"

Jill looked quickly to Joe, who motioned for her to begin.

"I just don't understand how we got to this place. I really thought we both wanted the same thing, but it's obvious to me that I'm really the only one who wants to see our family and marriage flourish. I work myself to the bone for this family with little to no help from anyone. I certainly don't think I ask for much, but all I get are kids who don't want to be with me or each other and a husband who tells me I should stop nagging and be thankful for all he has given to our family. All I am trying to do is help everyone be more of who they can be! Is that so terrible?"

Letting go of the familiar is hard, but results do not lie.

At this point, Joe craned his neck around his picture frame, attempting to enter the conversation.

"Yeah, Jill. That's right. Nothing and no one is ever good enough. No matter what I try to do for you, it will never be enough!"

This was obviously a well-worn path of conversation between the two. They both turned to me with the unspoken question, "Can you tell him/her what he/she needs to do to conform to my picture? Oh, I know it's partly my fault too, so can you tell me how I can more effectively *help* him/her conform to my picture?"

I don't care what counselors tell you about the beauty of a profession that enables you to help others. If we're honest, there are moments when we wonder if it's not too late to sign up for night school and become a plumber.

I have spent thousands of hours listening to stories similar to the fictional account above—stories told by disillusioned folks who have pictures in their minds of the ways they hoped life would be, but are living in a reality far from those desires. They bring with them a long history of fighting their reality using the same techniques over and over, with little to no success. Even though they know those methods aren't working, they are not ready to release them. I get that. Letting go of the familiar is hard, but results do not lie. After clients share how they have coped with their disappointments by attempting to corral and control people and circumstances into their desired outcome, I often ask, "How has that been working for you?" I don't ask that question sarcastically, even though the answer may be obvious. I ask because in order to be open to a new path toward change, we must be willing to name what is not working.

I would like to ask the same question to you, but instead of hearing my voice, I want you to hear the gentle voice of your Heavenly Father whispering to your weary heart, "How's that been working for you? Are you done yet? Are you?"

"Done with what?" you may ask. Done with believing that if you try harder, you can have that beautiful picture. Oh, I know—we all think we have outgrown the futility of trying to make life work our way. We scoff at quotes like this one attributed to Ralph Waldo Emerson: "Once you make a decision, the universe conspires to make it happen."

"I'm sorry, Mr. Emerson," you say, "but exactly what universe do you live in? Definitely not mine, that's for sure. In my universe, all forces work against me all the time. Allow me to introduce you to my laundry pile. And my inbox. And my children." We know Emerson's statement is wrong—*we know it*—because our experience tells us it's wrong. And yet, we are shocked when things don't go our way.

"No I'm not!" you may protest. "I know things don't usually go as planned. Tell me something I don't know!" But let's be honest. When things go badly—from traffic to whiny children to days when you feel as though there is a plot to destroy anything you are attempting to accomplish—do you not sometimes depart from your normal way of behaving? Do you become a different kind of person with a harsher tone of voice? Do you tend to say things you later regret? The universe is not cooperating with your definition of how it is supposed to operate, and you go a little crazy. One definition of crazy is "a departure from normal or desired behavior," and boy, do we depart.

Just in case you are under the impression that counselors are all shining examples of emotional and spiritual health, let me invite you into my world.

It was a Saturday. I had two goals, only two: return a can of paint to the paint store and buy some barstools at an antique shop. These were not lofty goals—it's not like I wanted to run a marathon or race to the top of a pyramid scheme; I just wanted to run a couple of errands. So, I arrived at the paint store, opened my car door, and out leapt—and I do mean leapt—the can of paint onto the pavement, bursting upon impact. Most of the paint—white paint, I might add—exploded underneath my black car. The underside of my car and a good portion of the parking lot were now covered in white paint. *Terrific.*

I took the walk of shame into the paint store, waited in line, and then mumbled, "Paint spill in the parking lot. It's a big one too." The employee enacted Operation Paint Spill Protocol because apparently I am not the first person to have a can of paint jump out of her vehicle completely unprovoked. I knew no set paint spill protocol for my car, however. The white mural—abstract style, of course— remains on my car's undercarriage to this day, unbeknownst to my husband, who I always insist drive because you can't see the damage from that side of the car.

I departed the scene of the crime and headed to the antique store, determined to check the second item off of my to-do list despite my disastrous start. I spotted two perfect cane-bottomed barstools. I sat down on one to check the comfort level, only to find myself completely sunken through the seat, which had broken upon impact. The first thought that came to my mind was *hide.* Hide anywhere. You must not be seen like this. Run out of the store, stool attached, and then sneak back later and destroy the video footage because you know the security guys will have a field day with this one. "Play it again, Frank! *She's actually wearing the barstool!*"

I wanted to crawl into a hole and never come out. It would need to be a large hole, what with the barstool attached to my rear end and all.

Needless to say, I lost it. See, I had a picture of how I thought my day should go. I had a picture of the role I would play in my day. I had intended to play the part of the woman who gets things done—the woman who writes things down like she's supposed to, who makes a plan, and then works the plan like a pro. This woman surely would have known to put the paint can in a box, and she never would have carelessly thrown the paint can in the back of her car. She definitely would have checked the weight limit before she sat on an antique stool. She would have been under the weight limit too.

I had a picture of how my day should go, but unlike Emerson's inspirational quote, the universe did not cooperate. My reality was nowhere near what I dreamed it should be, and instead of being the idealized me, I was still just me—the woman who acts first, thinks second, and then wants to run away from the mess she has made before anyone finds out.

What would make me act that way? What would cause me to behave like a crazy person? I'm a counselor, after all, and I know you're not supposed to hide things from your husband, and I know that if you destroy property you should confess and pay for it. I know these things, but what made me behave in a manner contrary to what I know? When the reality of my life does not match the picture in my head, I become hitched to the crazy train. I believe that I can control the people and circumstances in my life and force them into what I want them to be. It is this belief that drives my foolish behavior of hiding, telling half-truths, and losing it, of crying because I don't think my husband will accept someone who explodes paint all over her car and wears barstools.

What makes you crazy? What makes you say or do things that, even as you are saying them, even as you're doing them, you know you are going to regret them later? Is it when you host Christmas dinner for all the family, and you're determined for the day to match the picture in your head, no matter how many times it hasn't lived up to your expectations in the past? No matter how many times you burn the pie? No matter how many times your family gathering looks more like *The Jerry Springer Show* than Mayberry? You keep trying to create holiday bliss by working harder ahead of time and planning no-fail family Christmas activities and cooking the perfect green bean casserole, thinking, *Surely it will work this time.* But it never does. And with the sting of failure still fresh in your memory, you reach for your January copy of your favorite magazine and flip straight to the article entitled, "The New You in the New Year," vowing once again to try harder.

Why do we do this? Why do we continue to fall for the false promise of a shiny, perfect dream life? We long for paradise because we were created for paradise. We were created to live in an environment that cooperates with, not fights against, our desires. We were created for Eden, a place we've never been, and so we desire a perfect life full of healthy relationships.

Created for Eden

Desire was created by God before people ever sinned. Adam and Eve had desires and were entirely dependent upon God to grant them their desires. They never experienced need because their needs were immediately met. Their environment cooperated with their desires. Can you even imagine?

God just had one command, though, one directive: "You are free to eat from any tree in the garden; but you must not eat from the tree of the knowledge of good and evil, for when you eat from it you will certainly die" (Genesis 2:16–17). Isn't it interesting that God didn't explain how or why they would die? If I told one of my kids not to touch an apple, the first question they would ask would be, "Why? Is there, like, poison in it? Explain it to me." They would want me to explain myself to them because if they understood why, then they wouldn't have to trust. God doesn't tell Adam and Eve why. He tells them absolutely nothing. He set it up so they would have to trust in order to obey, rather than agree in order to obey.

Fast forward to Genesis 3 and the serpent is planting a seed of distrust in the woman's heart. "'You will not certainly die,' the serpent said to the woman. 'For God knows that when you eat from it your eyes will be opened, and you will be like God, knowing good and evil'" (vv. 4–5). Listen to the language of desire in Eve's response: "When the woman saw that the fruit of the tree was good for food and pleasing to the eye, and also desirable for gaining wisdom, she took some and ate it. She also gave some to her husband, who was with her, and he ate it" (v. 6).

At first blush, you would think that desire gave birth to sin. Therefore, if we can cut out desire, then we won't sin. But wait—not so fast. The desire was actually in Eve *before* she ever bit the fruit. It can't be desire that was the problem because Eve was created perfectly. So where was the breakdown? Eve's sin was rooted in her doubt in the goodness of God. What the serpent offered her was a way to circumvent God. He might as well have said, "Yes, yes, yes, you've got everything you need, but do you really know how long He's going to keep this up? This childlike thing you have with God, it's fine for now, but come on—you're a grown-up! It's time to take care of your own desires. You don't have to be dependent on anybody or anything to decide what you need and how you're going to get it. *Eat.*"

And with the first signs of doubt in her heart, Eve took a bite.

The pattern of the first sin and of every other sin since is this: not desire then sin but desire, *doubt*, sin. The problem is not desire; it's doubt.

Each day, you carry around a picture of how you long for life to be. This picture is comprised of people (yourself included) and circumstances. In and of themselves, there is probably nothing wrong with your picture because more than likely, it is connected back to your original design in Eden. The picture you have in your head of a beautiful relationship with your friend that's now been fractured is a product of your innate desire to be known and unashamed. Your frustration over your job that never gets done, no matter how hard you work, springs from the fact that in Eden, man had dominion over creation, and creation cooperated 100 percent of the time. There were no leaf blowers in Eden; there were no thorns and thistles. There was no such thing as a muffin top, a bad hair day, a hot flash, or mosquito bites.

And somehow, though we were never there, we remember it. *And we long for it.*

So when I experience a broken relationship, something inside of me hurts; when someone dies, a part of me dies because *it's not supposed to be this way.* Somehow, in some weird way, I live with the memory of a place I've never been. Those pictures you hold of the intimate marriage, the satisfying work, the healthier body, the successful children—they are all rooted back to Eden. When we suppress our God-given desires, we fight against our very design.

From Desires to Demands

All too often, our desires can become demands. We stare at our pictures; we focus all our energy on them. Our pictures grow bigger and bigger in importance until what we want becomes what we need and what we need becomes that by which we define our lives. We even answer the common question, "How are you doing?" in terms of our pictures.

"How has it been going?" I ask my clients.

"Great. We've been getting along better."

"I'm feeling hopeful. I got called in for a second interview."

All too often, our day is only as good as the degree to which reality matches our pictures. Let me say that again: *All too often, our day is only as good as the degree to which reality matches our pictures.*

All too often, our day is only as good as the degree to which reality matches our pictures.

Take, for instance, this popular statement about happy—no, let's just call it what it is—codependent mothers: "Every mother is only as happy as her least happy child." That would be precious, except it is a perfect example of what it looks like to be hitched to the crazy train. You might say, "My picture includes a happy child—is that so wrong?" No. That is not wrong. Of course that's what you want. But if you drop into despair and behave in ways you don't want to behave whenever your child is unhappy, then your desire is no longer just a desire; it is something you demand from others and even from God. When you write a scathing email to another parent because her kid was mean to your kid at school, when you bad mouth the coach because your child didn't make the team, when you can't sleep at night because your child is having a hard time making friends, your desire for your child's happiness is not just a desire anymore. Even though you ultimately have no control over the happiness of your child, your emotional, spiritual, and physical stability have become attached to it, and that, my friend, is crazy.

So, here's my question: How's that been working for you? Are you done yet?

I know what you're thinking: "OK, here we go. I'm ready. She's going to say that if I have enough faith, then I can rise above it all, stand in the chaos of a very broken world, and cheerfully sing a

Christian version of "Don't Worry, Be Happy." I'll then get inspired and start a blog called "Life Outside the Picture." After all, that's the kind of person I want to be."

Really? Tell me something: That might be who you want to be, but when you're hurting, is that the kind of person you want to have a cup of coffee with? I know I don't. When I'm hurting, I want to be in the presence of someone who has been there. Someone who gets it.

The One Who Understands

Jesus got it. The man of sorrows was familiar with suffering and radiated empathy, even though He knew how the story would end. Take Lazarus, for instance. Jesus wept over his death, even though He knew He was going to raise him (John 11:17–44). Why? Why would He be greatly troubled if He knew that in just a few seconds, Lazarus would breathe again? Because Jesus knew it was never supposed to be this way. Sisters shouldn't bury brothers. Relationships are meant to last forever.

Or take Jesus' plea to His Father in the hours before He was arrested. Jesus labored in prayer, sweating drops of blood as He petitioned His Father to "take this cup from me." If there was any other way, Jesus asked for it. But if not . . . He surrendered to God's will (see Luke 22:42). Usually when we tell this story, we emphasize the part "Yet not my will, but yours be done," but we can't truly connect with this statement of submission if we miss how Jesus reveals that what is coming is hard, and He would like to avoid it if at all possible. If we skip over "Is there any other way?" we characterize Jesus as someone who is not bothered by the pain of life, and we think that is how we are meant to be too. We feel shame because that's not who we are.

"Is there another way?" Here we see a High Priest who can sympathize with our weaknesses (Hebrews 4:15)—who gives us permission to be weak—because He felt weak. He was beaten, despised, rejected, and misunderstood. He bore the weight of the brokenness of the world not with a sunny disposition but with sweat and tears and at times, fury.

"Your will be done" holds a lot more weight when we hear it spoken not through unrealistic optimism but through pain because we know what it cost Him to say it.

"Your will be done" holds a lot more weight when we hear it spoken not through unrealistic optimism but through pain because we know what it cost Him to say it.

That picture you have? That desire that won't go away? Just because it is not your present reality does not mean it's wrong. The fact that God is in control does not mean you have to apologize for your pain and disappointment.

"I shouldn't want a spouse. Jesus is enough."

"My family is always going to be a dysfunctional mess. Why did I think this holiday would be any different?"

"It's unrealistic to think I can be close to my teenager."

No. Of course your desires are valid. Because you are created in God's image, you long for what is right and good, and you hurt when it is not. Of course you want companionship. Of course you want to connect with your family. Of course you want a holiday that is merry and bright. Of course you don't want the cancer to return. Of course you want to get the job. *Of course.* If you think your desires are wrong—the desires that actually reflect your design— you will hide and not discuss your longings with God. You will think if He knew what you really wanted, He would be mad at you. This perspective could not be further from the truth because He knows what it's like to hurt when faced with a reality that is different from what He desired it to be.

Stop hiding. Stop shaming. Come into the light.

The brokenness of life hurts because you were not designed for it, and while the painful weight of life is not optional, you do get to choose how you will carry that weight. You get to decide how you will engage with it. Just like physical weight lifting at the gym, the way you carry the weight of life will either strengthen you or injure you and take you out of the game.

How weary are you? How are you carrying the weight of reality outside of your picture? Be honest in your answer; take a minute to feel the burden of your weariness. It's kind of unbearable, isn't it?

Come to me, all you who are weary
and burdened, and I will give you rest.
Take my yoke upon you and learn from me,
for I am gentle and humble in heart,
and you will find rest for your souls.
For my yoke is easy and my burden is light.
—Matthew 11:28–30

When Jesus gave this invitation to His Hebrew listeners, He was well aware of the heavy, self-righteous burden the Pharisees and other religious leaders had placed on the people through the unobtainable expectations of the law. Like an ox forced to plow a field with a heavy weight on its back, the Jews had been struggling to plow the field of life underneath an impossible standard. Jesus knew they were weary from their efforts that could never be good enough. He was offering a better way—the *only* way to have peace with God and finally find rest. Jesus' yoke—His grace-filled teaching and gentle care that never leaves you to plow alone—was a stark, beautiful contrast to the weight of the law that left the people exhausted and disheartened.

Jesus extends this invitation to us today, but it is not an open invitation. The rest that Jesus offers comes with a very high cost: in order to receive Jesus' light and easy yoke, you must be willing to lay down your own. You have been plowing the field with a terribly heavy burden. You've been living life your own way, following your own agenda. Your yoke must go in order to receive the yoke Jesus offers. You can't wear both, and He will not force His yoke upon you. He says, "Take it . . . but before you take it, you have to lay down your own."

Are you weary enough to lay your burden down?

We're kind of like the toddler who insists on tying his own shoelaces, even though he is developmentally incapable of doing so. His mother watches him struggle, and although she knows that she could storm over and demand, "Oh, just let me do it—we're in a hurry," the loving thing to do would be to patiently wait until he is so weary of trying that he is ready to receive help.

"Are you done yet?" his mom might ask with a smile, as she bends over to weave the laces with experienced hands.

Jesus tenderly asks, "Are you done yet? Are you done carrying the burden of trying to attain your perfect picture? Of trying to make life 'work'?" And as He asks, He also waits with skilled hands, ready to catch your burden as you shrug it to His feet, ready to give you the deep rest your soul has always longed for. This process is painful; the cost is high, but the rest you were designed for is worth it. "Come to Me," He says.

You may be completely ensnared in the trap of worshipping your picture. *Come.*

You may be disillusioned and cynical, scarred by those who were supposed to love you well, and you just don't trust Him. *Come.*

You may be scared to death because you don't know Him well enough to believe He knows *you* well enough to know what you really need. *Come.*

How weary are you? Are you done yet? He sees you. Come to Him—it's time.

Process Questions

1. What does your picture look like? It may help to think of your picture in terms of segments, such as family, job, friendships, etc.

_____

_____

_____

_____

2. As you clarify your picture, what emotions are evoked? Fear? Hope? Pain? Despair?

_____

_____

_____

_____

3. Can you identify the ways in which you have become weary by trying to achieve your picture?

_____

_____

_____

_____

4. How have you tried to shame or deny your picture (deaden your desire)?

_____

_____

_____

_____

5. Like Eve demonstrated in Genesis 3, it is our doubt in God's goodness and provision that causes us to behave in ways we later regret. Take a moment to consider the false beliefs about God that led to your responses in questions 3 and 4. Write out a prayer of confession, not for your responses, but for what you believed about God that caused you to respond as you did.

_____

_____

_____

_____

6. The Father is asking you, "Are you tired enough to abandon your own yoke and come under Mine?" Write your response as a prayer.

_____

_____

_____

_____

Chapter 2

If It Is to Be, It's Up to Me

The Path of Unbelief

My husband had a dream of taking our family of five to Europe. He saved every frequent flyer mile of his entire career to make that dream a reality. As he pored over travel books, I pled with him to think reasonably. The children were 17, 12, and 9 at the time. Any mom can see the problem. We couldn't even agree on which movie to watch in our own basement. Why should we travel to another continent and spend thousands of dollars when we could just argue at home for free? I fought the plan with every fiber of my being, but here's the strange thing: I didn't fight it because I didn't want to go. Actually, the opposite was true. I wanted to go as badly as my husband did. But I wouldn't allow myself to hope for anything that was so far outside my control. Such hopes put me in too vulnerable of a position. In my opinion, it was best to whittle those dreams down to a comfortable reality . . . three days in Disney—*maybe*—but anything beyond that was just asking for disappointment. Unfazed by my pessimism, my husband booked the flights.

Three months later, my family and I sat in the airport, waiting to board our flight to Paris. Scenes of angry mobs setting fire to buildings and overturning cars flashed across the television monitor. You have three guesses as to where those scenes were taking place. Travel advisories streamed before our eyes as images of Paris in a state of dangerous chaos dominated the screen. We had not even begun our dream trip, and it was already going awry. My inner dialogue began:

"Did I not tell him this was a bad idea? Of course one of the worst civil upheavals in decades strikes the week the Sparkmans are coming to town. *Of course.* Why am I not surprised? The same thing happened on our honeymoon in Hawaii. Record typhoons hit the islands just as we did. I could make a fortune predicting disasters because I could just pick the time and location of our vacations. Oh, man. I know what's coming. Public transportation will be completely shut down, but it won't really matter because everything we have so carefully planned to see will be closed anyway. Forget the Louvre and the Eiffel Tower; the five of us will spend our European holiday in a cramped hotel room arguing over which French movies to watch. Is it too late to cash in our travel insurance?"

My fuming reverie was interrupted by the final boarding call. I glared at my husband as we walked toward the gate. I didn't have to say a word; he knew the look. *I. Told. You. So.*

I know I'm not alone in my protective strategy of not allow-ing my hopes to move beyond what I feel I can control. We all size the gap between our reality and our desired picture of reality. Our response to that gap is the truest statement of our theology. It reveals the identity we really ascribe to. We will either believe we are well-provided-for children of the King or we will, like Eve before us, listen to the whisper of the enemy who tells us we are orphans, on our own to do whatever we must do to get the life we think we need. It is here, when we face this gap, that we see where our hope truly lies.

Child of the King or orphan. Belief or unbelief.

Our Orphan Mentality

The gaps are endless. You want your child to love Jesus, but he's indifferent. You desire to play with your grandchildren, but your body is weakened by old age. You want to own a successful business, but you're about to file for bankruptcy. You long for a peaceful home, but your children fight constantly. You crave connection with your spouse, but there seems to be a brick wall between you. And on and on. When we see these gaps, we often forget our true identity as heirs and respond as orphans, thinking, *If it's to be, it's up to me. I must take care of my desires because if I don't, no one else will.* We become Eve all over again, not only picturing for ourselves what we need but also determining how we are going to make that picture come true. In our orphan mentality our picture changes from what we would *like* to have to what we *must* have in order to be happy and satisfied. At this point, our picture has dropped sideways, grown wheels, and we are now hitched to what has become the crazy train. We are now consumed by our attempts to corral and control people and circumstances as if our very lives depended upon it because we think they actually do.

Isaiah 30:15–16 clearly lays out this orphan mentality: "In repentance and rest is your salvation, in quietness and trust is your strength, but you would have none of it. . . . You said, 'We will ride off on swift horses.'" God is speaking to the nation of Judah as they face their enemies, exhorting them to look to Him for provision and protection. He is grieved that they didn't. He is saying, "All you had to do was trust Me, and you would have been safe. But you wouldn't do it. You took matters into your own hands and set about saving yourselves."

Adam and Eve, Judah, me, you . . . instead of accepting the rest God offers through His provision, we stiff arm Him and look

> *We seek to make our lives work apart from God, and this unbelief drives all the sinful actions we will ever commit.*

instead to our own resources to create the life we think we must have. We seek to make our lives work apart from God, and this unbelief drives all the sinful actions we will ever commit.

When we believe it is up to us to fulfill our pictures of how our lives should look, we are adhering to the orphan mentality. Depending on our particular circumstances at a given time, this mentality will be manifest in one of two ways: we will be a resolver, or we will be a victim.

Resolver

Resolvers are the can-do people with a plan for everything. They know how to get it done. They have the tutors, the counselors, the seminars, the books, the apps. Life isn't matching the picture? The right resource can close the gap, bringing people and circumstances exactly where they belong. It's all about making good choices. Work the plan, and you can create the life you want.

Lest you think this viewpoint is limited to the secular world, take a stroll down the aisles of a Christian bookstore. You will see book after book promising *Seven Steps to an Intimate Marriage* or *Twelve Days to Taming the Tongue*. Resolvers read these books cover to cover, frantically taking notes.

Resolvers often drive their families crazy by trying to create an unattainable goal of "special." They may force family fun nights and command everyone to have a good time. A friend of mine once ordered her teenaged son to play a card game with her, even though he didn't want to play and had repeatedly said no. He said, "Mom, are you actually forcing me to play a game with you? Are you seriously trying to do that?" Despite how crazy she knew she sounded, she stuck to her guns because her latest parenting book told her that in order to improve her relationship with her son, they needed to have fun, shared experiences.

"Yes, I am making you play a game with me. Now, deal."

You can imagine how fun and successful that bonding time was.

As a recovering resolver myself, I must confess that for every one plan I have for myself, I have four for everyone else in my life. I have an answer to the problem before people even know they have a problem. Just ask my family. I thought I was being a visionary wife and mom, cheering and coaching my people to be the best versions of themselves, but come to find out, it's dangerous to have a plan for someone else's life.

"I only want what's best for you!" I once said to my daughter. "I think you have so much to give. How could I not want more for you when I see your potential?"

"That's just it, Mom. You always think I can do better. I'm never enough for you."

Ouch. I had hitched myself to my child's potential, and I hadn't even realized it. Not only was I unaware of the damage I was doing to her but also I truly believed I was doing the right thing. I thought I was being a responsible, engaged mother. Instead, I was corralling and controlling her into my picture of who she should be.

I was troubled by my daughter's words, but can I be honest? I was also a tad bit resentful. I thought, *Why doesn't this family appreciate all I do for them? And why isn't my husband helping me? Can't he see I am running myself ragged? If only he would read that book on biblical manhood I so thoughtfully surprised him with last Valentine's Day! But, no* (said with a sigh as I wipe the perspiration off my forehead). *It's clear I'm the only one who really cares. The only one trying. If this family is going to be all*

We can learn a lot by listening to others share how they experience us.

that God wants it to be, it is up to me to make that happen.

When life matches my picture, my resolver self is a happy camper, cheerful, and loving. But when people and circumstances do not cooperate, my mood drastically changes. Remember, crazy is defined as a sharp departure from normal or *desired* behavior. In these circumstances, I often respond with emotional, irrational intensity. I am so dependent upon my picture for life that it might as well be my oxygen tank and someone is standing on my air tube. I am desperate to get them off so I can breathe again. I can behave crazy to the extent that my daughter once said, "Mama, when you get like this, you remind me of Cinderella's stepmother."

Ouch again. Teaching your children to be emotionally articulate can really come back to bite you.

We can learn a lot by listening to others share how they experience us. As painful as it was to hear, I wish I had listened to my daughter's description of me in that candid moment. Jesus was speaking through her honest words, beckoning me off the crazy train. Instead, I chose to stiff arm Him and ride off on my own version of a swift horse. As a committed resolver, I kept working the plan. And working. And working. But it wasn't working. The harder I tried to corral and control my family, the lonelier and angrier I became. I started to lose hope.

The realization that the resources we possess apart from Christ will never be enough to get the life we think we need can be a watershed moment, propelling us resolvers to embrace our need for Jesus and run to Him. But if we continue to live with an orphan mentality, we have no other choice than to shut down—to become a victim.

Victim

What does unbelief look like in a victim's response to the gaps in their lives? As a proactive person, I have a strong negative reaction to the word *victim*. Yet that is exactly what we often become when resolving has not worked. We can become cynical and hard. Outwardly, this might look a lot like passivity. For example, I have counseled countless Christian men whose wives dragged them into my office to complain about their lack of spiritual leadership. These men sit on my couch, heads hung low, eyes averted, waiting for me to join in on the verbal barrage. They are not lacking in knowledge. They have been to the weekend seminars, read the books, and participated in the accountability groups. They are well aware of the often-crippling expectations the Christian culture can place on them. No, the problem is rarely a lack of knowledge; after all, any man who has been in church for at least one Father's Day has heard plenty on the need for men to step it up. While women receive carnations and standing ovations on Mother's Day, men are given a list of things they need to do better. But knowledge taught without a strong emphasis on our desperate need for the power of Christ becomes an unbearable, unsustainable weight, so it's easier to just check out.

The victim's hope still lies in the attainment of their picture, but unlike the resolver who still thinks they can get their picture, the victim's hope is depleted because they have experienced disappointment one too many times. Victims succumb to either despairing shame—"It's my fault. I shouldn't want it anyway"—or blame—"It's your fault I don't have what I want."

Remember my family's dream-turned-nightmare Paris vacation? I had a stereotypical victim's response. History had shown me my desire (a happy family vacation) might not happen, so I suppressed my desire. I shamed it. I shamed my husband for having his dream.

Vulnerability is the pathway to feeling our need for Jesus, to remembering we are actually children of the King.

"What are you thinking? Why would we do that? Don't you know how bad this could be?" Contrary to what I was saying, I actually wanted to beg, "Please argue with me. Please tell me I'm wrong," because I wanted that happy family vacation more than anything. Yet, I was too afraid to hope. I was too scared to say what I really wanted, so I shut my heart down.

When our orphan mentality takes on the attitude of a victim, we suppress and shame our desires because longing makes us vulnerable, and vulnerability is scary because we cannot guarantee that we will get what we long for. Being willing to name and own our pictures just feels too risky. So we numb. We become passive. We are cynical toward life. Our posture is a stiff, soundproof wall, silencing our aching hearts that cry out for connection. I wanted Paris; my crossed arms and harsh tone said otherwise.

The resolver and the victim: two children of the King who live out of an orphan mentality by either taking full responsibility for their desires and trying to force people and circumstances into their pictures or by resigning that they will never be provided for anyway, so what's the point of wanting anything at all? Both resolver and victim are terrified of vulnerability, yet vulnerability is the pathway to feeling our need for Jesus, to remembering we are actually children of the King.

What have you been doing with your desires? Are you the resolver who controls and corrals or the victim who shames and blames? Are you both? What parts of your life—what parts of others' lives—are you trying to control? What parts of your heart have you tried to shut down?

Let's go back to the Garden of Eden. When Adam and Eve chose to believe that only they, not God, could fulfill their desires, they ate, and then they hid. They were resolvers: "He's holding out on us. Let's pursue pleasure and power on our terms." And then they were victims caught up in shame, "Please don't look at me!" and then blaming, "She made me do it!" And so it has been sin's pattern ever since: desire, unbelief, disobedience, shame.

As predictable as the pattern of sin, so is the pattern of redemption. God initiated reconciliation with Adam and Eve: "Where are you?" Of course, He knew exactly where they were; this had nothing to do with location and everything to do with His gentle, patient pursuit. In the Garden we hear the heart of a Father asking His children, "How did you get here? What lie did you believe that caused you to do what you did? Where is your heart?"

And so He asks us. "Where are you? What desires have you stopped trusting Me with? What are you demanding from life and others because you don't really believe that I am good or that I will give you My best? When did you stop believing that I will provide for you, so much so that you decided it would be better to numb your heart than to have a longing go unfulfilled? *Where are you?*"

He finds us, of course, because He has known where we are all along. He pulls us out of the bushes of shame, discards our flimsy fig leaves, and covers us with the sacrificial atonement of Christ. Creation, fall, redemption, restoration. We get to experience the gospel over and over again.

Resolvers, *He's calling to you*, so unclench your fists. If your hope for yourself is Jesus in you and your hope for others is Jesus in them, then you don't have to be afraid; you don't have to let fear drive you to control people and situations. You can be free to desire great things for yourself and others but not demand them on your terms.

Victims, *He sees you*. You can afford to hope because the One who owns the cattle on a thousand hills (Psalm 50:10) is footing the bill, and He desires good things for you. He does. And you can afford to let others see you, *really see you,* because grace has covered your shame.

We are orphans no more. Our provision is covered by our Father who lavishes us with a perfect, pure, and fierce love. It is not enough to know this in our heads; we must fight to walk in this truth moment by moment.

Process Questions

1. As defined in this lesson, how does someone with an orphan mentality respond to the gap between their picture and their reality?

_____

_____

_____

_____

2. Do you tend to behave as a resolver or a victim? What are some examples from your life where you can clearly see yourself taking on one or both of these roles?

_____

_____

_____

_____

3. Meditate on Isaiah 30:15–18. What words or phrases seem to jump out at you? What are some examples of swift horses in your life, meaning, things you are tempted to look to for hope and rescue?

_____

_____

_____

_____

4. A pattern was established in Genesis 3 of desire, unbelief, disobedi-ence, and shame. Describe a time you walked through this pattern. (Example: "My desire was _____, I didn't believe _____ about God's character, I disobeyed in this way, my sin was exposed, and I responded to my shame like this . . .")

_____

_____

_____

_____

5. Meditate on the truth that because of Christ's salvation, you are no longer an orphan but His child. Ask God to move this promise from your head to your heart.

_____

_____

_____

_____

Chapter 3

Leaving the Old Yoke Behind

Step One: Come

*Come to me, all you who are weary
and burdened, and I will give you rest.
Take my yoke upon you
and learn from me,
for I am gentle and humble in heart,
and you will find rest for your souls.
For my yoke is easy
and my burden is light.*

—Matthew 11:28–30

How often have we run to these verses in our weariness and felt relieved? The truth is, this passage makes us feel better. Peaceful. Taken care of—until we realize what Jesus is really saying. The call offers a choice we must make again and again. What does that choice entail?

EXPOSURE

Between My Realit

Unbelief
Orphan

"In repentance and rest is your salvation, in quietness and trust is your strength, but you would have none of it . . . You said, 'We will ride off on swift horses.'" Isaiah 30:15–16

Resolver

Hope in the attainment of the picture through personal efforts.

corralling

controlling

Victim

Hope in the attainment of the picture, but that hope is now depleted. Result is: shame (my fault) or blame (other's or God's fault)

disengaged/passive

cynical (shame picture)

hardened heart (shuts down desire)

# of a GAP
nd My Picture

Belief
Son/Daughter

"Come to me, all you who are weary and burdened, and I will give you rest. Take my yoke upon you and learn from me, for I am gentle and humble in heart and you will find rest for your souls. For my yoke is easy and my burden is light." Matthew 11:28–30

Come

Repent of how you have sought to make life work apart from Him. "Against you, you only, have I sinned and done what is evil in your sight." Psalm 51:4

Take His Yoke

Surrender to His larger picture and "put on the lenses" of:

A. He is in this.

"In all things God works for the good of those who love him, who have been called according to his purpose." Romans 8:28

B. He is in me.

"His divine power has given us everything we need for a godly life through our knowledge of him who called us by his own glory and goodness." 2 Peter 1:3

Learn from Him

As we commune with the Lord, in prayer and the Word, He molds our hearts to His.

"Take delight in the LORD, and he will give you the desires of your heart." Psalm 37:4

Rest

To be free from effort that does not satisfy as we continue to focus on His larger picture beyond our own.

"So we fix our eyes not on what is seen, but on what is unseen, since what is seen is temporary, but what is unseen is eternal." 2 Corinthians 4:18

As this chart illustrates, when we are faced with a gap between our reality and our picture of what we desire reality to be, we must choose between unbelief and belief. Orphan or heir. When we choose the path of unbelief, we continue to labor under our own heavy yoke, trying to make life work apart from intimate communion with Christ.

Jesus invites us to a whole new way of life, the path of belief, comprised of the four essential steps you see in the Exposure of a Gap chart:

1. Come
2. Take His Yoke
3. Learn from Him
4. Rest

We're going to walk through these steps over the course of the rest of this book, but before we dive in, let me be clear that this process is indeed a new way of doing life. In Matthew 11, Jesus does not lay out a one-time path but one we have to choose each and every time we are faced with life outside of our picture. While the path may become clearer the more we walk it, it is nonetheless a hard one. It involves death to self. It will involve pain. Sin will still pull at us, beckoning us to go our own way, but because of what Christ has done for us, we have the capacity to make the choice to live out of our true identity and rest in His care.

The first step of belief is to come to Jesus. We have already explored the call to come to Him, no matter how or why we're coming. We've turned toward Jesus and considered what He has to say about our efforts, our anxiety, and our exhaustion. But what does coming to Jesus really entail? What does it actually mean?

Coming to our Savior does not mean asking Him to squeeze into our lives that are already full to overflowing with our own efforts. "I think I've got a spot riiiiight here, Jesus. Make Yourself comfortable, but be careful not to crowd out my self-sufficiency, OK?" To come to Jesus is to lay down our own burdensome yoke, our attempts to make life work apart from Him. To come is to repent. We must repent of not believing in His goodness and power—the unbelief that caused us to hitch to the crazy train in the first place.

Coming to our Savior does not mean asking Him to squeeze into our lives that are already full to overflowing with our own efforts.

King David, the only person ever referred to as "a man after God's own heart" (1 Samuel 13:14), dug himself into such a deep hole. He had every luxury right at his fingertips but decided God's generous provision was not enough. Looking out his window one night, David saw Bathsheba, the wife of one of his top soldiers. He was lonely. She was lovely. David was well aware of the commands he was about to break, but he chose to believe that he, not God, was the one to be trusted with his desires. The root of his sin was not a lack of knowledge or even a lack of self-control; it was unbelief. Disregarding God's commands, he placed Bathsheba in the center of his picture and believed he had to have her. His desire became his need, so he was going to do whatever he had to do to make his picture his reality. He committed adultery with her, which might have been easy enough to cover up, but she became pregnant. This was a real problem since her husband Uriah was off at war, where King David should have been in the first place.

David was a quick thinker, so he sent orders for Uriah to come home. He encouraged Uriah to spend some time with his wife, but Uriah refused to leave his post, the king's presence. Plans foiled, David went to extreme measures to cover up his sin. He sent Uriah to the front lines and ordered the soldiers behind him to fall back, guaranteeing that Uriah would be killed in battle and, more importantly, silenced. (See 2 Samuel 11.)

That is some serious crazy train stuff, right there. David took the wife of one of his best men and then had that good man killed, all because he was convinced that in order to have his ideal life picture fulfilled, he must have Bathsheba. David behaved like a prodigal son, taking the blessings his father had given him—status and wealth—and using them to chase his picture of how life should be.

David had a case of spiritual amnesia. Peter speaks of this ailment in 2 Peter 1. After listing qualities indicative of spiritual growth (goodness, knowledge, self-control, perseverance, godliness, mutual affection, and love), he cautions, "But whoever does not have them is nearsighted and blind, *forgetting that they have been cleansed from their past sins*" (v. 9, author's emphasis). David sinned, not because he didn't know any better or because he simply lacked self-control, but because he forgot He was a son of the King and jumped onto the path of unbelief. David's core desire for intimacy wasn't wrong, but he took his desire into his own hands. He doubted the goodness and provision of God. David believed that he, not God, was the best one to decide what he needed and how to get it. Though he knew God's laws about adultery and murder, his knowledge was not enforced by a belief that he could trust his Father over his own thinking. David's *unbelief* is what led to his sinful behavior.

He needed to repent. And if you read Psalm 51, you see David's repentant heart as he cries out for forgiveness.

The Godless Evangelical

Orphan-like unbelief and subsequent behavior are not usually as obvious as David's sins were. More often than not, they are much slower and subtler. For example, as Christians, we may do our best not to act ungodly, but hidden beneath our avoidance of outward sins is something just as dangerous. In our attempts to avoid ungodly behavior, we can actually become godless. We can completely immerse ourselves in the Christian subculture, using the jargon and actions of faithful churchgoers, while living without a constant awareness of the movement and direction of God in our lives. Isaiah addresses this dangerous pitfall:

> *The Lord says:*
> *"These people come near to me*
> *with their mouth and honor me with their lips,*
> *but their hearts are far from me.*
> *Their worship of me is based on*
> *merely human rules they have been taught."*
> —Isaiah 29:13

What does this godless evangelicalism look like for us today? For my husband and me, it involved a decision to move to the big city. We were newly married, and we had a plan. It was a great plan we believed would lead us to our picture . . . a corporate job in a metropolitan area. But before my husband could reach that goal, he first had to put in his time by working as an engineer at a nuclear plant in a small town. I remember confidently telling our pastor about our well-laid plans:

"We won't be here for long. As soon as we can, we'll relocate to the city."

He lovingly responded, "So that's what you feel God would have you do?"

Crickets.

We forget we're His children, so we assume the role of an orphan and go it alone.

"Right. Well, um, actually, that's just what you do. You climb the ladder to bigger and better things. That's the American way."

At that point in our lives, we had been believers for years. We were leaders in our church, and yet, we had never even considered asking God *if* He wanted us to move to the city. No need, right? Our picture included us moving to the city, and our picture directed our prayers about moving.

"*When* we move, will You please provide a house?"

"*When* we move, will You help us make some friends?"

"*When* we move, will You help us find a great church?"

To pray, "*Should* we move?" would have rocked our picture, and not only did we not want to take that risk, we never even considered taking that risk.

It should caution us that we can be well-respected leaders in our Christian communities and not actively seek and depend on God for every aspect of our lives. It should be terrifying that we can talk and walk in spiritual circles without engaging with God Himself, without considering and experiencing the movement of God in our lives. It should be alarming that when my clients tell me about their pain and I ask them, "Where do you see God moving in this?" they often go mute because they've never even thought about it. I get that. When I'm faced with a difficult situation, it's difficult for me to see past my pain too.

God promises to always be with us, but we often fail to acknowledge His presence. We don't allow His presence to change, inform, or direct us. We forget we're His children, so we assume the role of an orphan and go it alone.

Adulterous David, the murderer. The godless evangelical. Both have forgotten who they are; both are called to come . . . to repent.

Remember and Repent

God moved David's heart that seemed so far away from Him to a place of repentance by speaking through his mentor, Nathan. What would you have said to David if he had been your friend?

"David! How could you? What were you thinking? Do you realize what is going to happen now because you blew it? You know better than this! Do we need to put you in some kind of accountability group to keep you from doing something like this again?"

Probably not the most helpful approach . . .

Thankfully, the truth of the gospel changes not only the way we repent of sin, but it also changes the way in which we call others to repentance.

The prophet Nathan was both wise and winsome in the way he confronted David. He told him a story of a rich man and a poor man. The rich man had many flocks, but the poor man only had one little ewe, which he loved very much and kept as a pet. One day the rich man held a feast for some guests, and instead of sacrificing one of his own sheep, he stole and slaughtered the poor man's one treasured sheep.

After listening to Nathan's story, David became enraged. Who would do such a thing? He demanded there be harsh repercussions for such a selfish act. And then, in a suspense-filled moment, Nathan revealed, *"You are the man."* Now if I were Nathan, I probably would have been tempted to gloat about my genius approach to a sticky situation, but I think it's pretty clear that Nathan's intentions were not to shame or to boast but to bring about conviction.

Then Nathan said to David,

"You are the man!

This is what the LORD, the God of Israel, says:

'I anointed you king over Israel,

and I delivered you from the hand of Saul.

I gave your master's house to you,

and your master's wives into your arms.

I gave you all Israel and Judah.

And if all this had been too little,

I would have given you even more.

Why did you despise the word of the LORD

by doing what is evil in His eyes?'"

—2 Samuel 12:7–9

God was asking David, "Why? Did you forget who you are? Did you forget who I am? I've given you everything, and I would have given you more. Why didn't you trust Me?"

Imagine this exhortation in today's context:

A mom notices that cash has been disappearing from her purse for a couple of weeks. One morning, she walks into the kitchen where her purse sits open on the counter. Her son's hands hold her wallet. She realizes, *Oh no, my son is the one who has been stealing from me!* Her son stares at her like a deer caught in the headlights and immediately gushes tears of remorse.

"I'm so sorry, Mom—I'm so sorry! I know it was wrong to take the money. It's just that I wanted this baseball glove so bad! But

I know it was wrong, and I'm going to pay you back double for everything I took. I'm so sorry, I'm so sorry, I'm so sorry!"

How would you respond if you were that mother? Would you downplay the seriousness of the act and jump straight to the consequences?

"Well! I'm glad to see that you understand, and yes, you certainly will pay me back double. Just remember this lesson, and don't do it again, OK?"

Or would your horror over your son's theft lead you to shame your son into right behavior?

"How could you do such a thing? You weren't raised like this! And yes, you will be working this debt off for a good long while to make sure you never do such a thing again!"

Both of these responses might address the behavior, but they don't get to the heart of the problem, which is the son's lack of trust in his mom's provision. This lack of trust—this unbelief in her love and care—is the real reason why this mother is hurt. It's the reason why we hurt when our own kids disobey. When this mom discovers that the one whom she has loved, provided for, and invested in for his entire life has been stealing from her, she should have one question on her mind: "Why? Why didn't you ask me? You're my son. Did you not trust that I would care for you? Did you forget who you are?"

This son's sin is personal to his mother, and our sin is personal to God. It indicates a breakdown not in knowledge or discipline but in relationship.

David's prayer of repentance in Psalm 51 reflects this relational foundation of sin as he is finally convicted of his unbelief and calls out to his Father, "Against you, you only, have I sinned and done what is evil in your sight" (v. 4).

Notice, when David humbly comes before God to ask for forgiveness, he never mentions his acts of adultery and murder. This

True repentance requires we repent of our unbelief in the gospel, because it's our unbelief that leads to our sinful behavior.

omission seems strange, but he's technically right not to name them. His hideous actions were the fruit of his sin, whereas the root of his sin was unbelief.

When we leave our yoke to come to Christ, it's not enough to confess our actions: "I'm sorry for yelling. I'm sorry for stealing. I'm sorry I bit the apple." True repentance requires we repent of our unbelief in the gospel, because it's our unbelief that leads to our sinful behavior.

All sin—*all*—is the result of failing to believe the gospel. We forget one or both of these two gospel tenets:

1. We are well-provided-for children of the King. We don't have to manipulate or steal because He promises to give us everything we need.

2. Our righteousness—our right standing before God—is in Christ alone. We didn't earn it, we can't lose it, and it can't be taken away from us.

In his article, "The Centrality of the Gospel," Tim Keller writes:

It is very common in the church to think as follows: "The gospel is for non-Christians. One needs it to be saved. But once saved, you grow through hard work and obedience." But Colossians 1:6 shows that this is a mistake. Both confession and "hard work" that is not arising from and in line with the gospel will not sanctify you–they will strangle you. All our problems come from a failure to apply the gospel.

The gospel is not just the pathway to saving faith; it is our lifeline for faithfully following Jesus. The truths of the gospel are what keep us from sin, so it is crucial we remember them.

You may be thinking, *Yes. Got it. I've been a Christian for a while now, so I am very well versed in the gospel.* But were you walking in the reality of the gospel today when you snapped at your child for dragging his feet when you were already late? When you gave your spouse the cold shoulder over dinner? When you micromanaged someone else's life, again? Why did you sin today? Which of these two aspects of the gospel did you not believe? I know you think you know the gospel, but are you aware of how frequently you forget it? If our knowledge of truth is going to set us free, then we have to make sure we really know how the gospel applies to our daily lives.

I often forget the gospel when I'm late to work in the mornings. Some might say I have what you could call an issue with punctuality. I'm embarrassed by this perceived fault. Tardiness is an especially bad trait if you are a counselor since keeping a client waiting is frowned upon in professional settings. I don't want to be seen as unprofessional, so I am tempted to paint myself in a different light. Upon ushering my clients back to my office, I apologize for the wait and complain about how bad the traffic was that morning. Now, I don't exactly say that the traffic made me late. That would be lying, and I know better. Instead, in an attempt to attain my picture of myself as a respectable counselor, I practice deception, which is, plain and simple, a socially acceptable form of lying. In that moment, I push aside the righteousness of Christ, which gives me the freedom to admit my faults, ask for forgiveness, and helps me to change, and instead put on "punctuality righteousness," a false attempt to keep my image intact. When I forget I wear the righteousness of Christ, I will do whatever I need to do—including lie—to hold on to my self-righteousness.

Me. The child who steals from his mother. The murderous adulterer. We are all in the same boat. We've forgotten the truths of the gospel.

You might say, "Come on, now. You cannot put yourself and your little white lie about traffic in the same boat as 'major offenders.'"

But it's true. When I forget what Christ has done for me, when I doubt His goodness, I will do whatever I need to do in order to buy back what I think I have lost. I will take matters into my own hands. I'll stretch the truth. Shame my child. Snap at my spouse. When I forget the beautiful truths of the gospel, I climb into the boat with David. And the stealing child. And any other person who has ever sinned. I take God's provisions and use them to make life work apart from Him. My sin is not an educational problem ("If only I had more theological training, I wouldn't make such poor choices!") or a volitional problem ("I just need to want holiness more"). It is a relational problem ("God, in this moment, I do not believe that You alone have made me righteous and that You will provide for me").

In his book *The Return of the Prodigal Son*, Henri Nouwen says:

I am the prodigal son every time I search for unconditional love where it cannot be found. . . . I keep taking the gifts that God has given me—my health, my intellectual and emotional gifts—and keep using them to impress people, receive affirmation and praise, and compete for rewards, instead of developing them for the glory of God. . . . It's almost as if I want to prove to myself and to my world that I do not need God's love, that I can make a life on my own, that I want to be fully independent.

Jesus says to us, "Come." He asks us to repent of our unbelief and leave behind our orphan way of life. We no longer have to fight for righteousness—our righteousness is in Him. We no longer have to corral and control to get what we think we must have—we are

Leaving the Old Yoke Behind

well-provided-for children. We no longer have to shut down our desires—He will be faithful to give us whatever we need. To come does not mean to be devoid of desire; instead, faith instructs us to hold our desires with open hands and entrust them to the Father who knows what we need.

My sin is not an educational problem or a volitional problem. It is a relational problem.

Belief is a moment-by-moment choice. What will you choose? Right now, even though your own efforts and self-righteousness may feel safe and insulating, they are actually suffocating your spiritual life and stealing your sanity. Will you choose belief instead?

Remember who you are. Repent of the unbelief that caused you to forget. Your Father is calling out to you, whispering your true name, your true identity. Do you hear Him? Lay down your yoke, repent of taking the path of unbelief, and come.

Process Questions

1. Read 2 Peter 1:3–11. Sin is a relational issue rooted in spiritual amnesia. What do we forget when we sin?

_____

_____

_____

_____

2. The gospel has two main tenets. If you are in Christ, what does the gospel say is true about you?

_____

_____

_____

_____

3. Think of a sin you've committed in the last day or two. When you disobeyed, which of the two gospel truths did you not believe? How did you relate to God in that moment? Confess your unbelief to your Father, and rest in His forgiveness.

_____

_____

_____

_____

4. Second Peter 1:3 says, "His divine power has given us everything we need for a godly life through our knowledge of him who called us by his own glory and goodness." Spend some time meditating on the truth of your secure identity in Him—the fact that you don't have to perform or earn your way to righteousness. How does that change the way you relate to Him? How does it change the way you relate to others?

_____

_____

_____

_____

Chapter 4

The Deadly Theology of Good Choices

Step Two: Take His Yoke

Have you ever strolled through the mall, minding your own business, when a heavenly scent stopped you in your tracks? You didn't come to the shopping center intending to eat a giant cinnamon roll, but your sense of smell overrides your muscle control. Before you know it, you're standing in front of a glass display of sugary goodness, transfixed. A platter of free samples sits on the counter with a sign saying, "Take one."

What do you do? You play out the possible scenarios. If you give in and consume the free sample, that choice will definitely lead to the inhalation of a not-so-free pastry the size of your face. You'll gain at least five pounds. You will awaken the sugar beast, and you won't be able to stop. Krispy Kreme at the gas station. Sugar Babies at the supermarket checkout. Entire cartons of ice cream eaten by the light of Netflix. This won't end well.

But if you resist, you'll be rewarded with a slimmer, healthier you. All the books tell you so. In an act of sheer will, you say no to the cinnamon roll, just like you've said no to so many treats before, thinking of the payout that is to come.

But what if you don't do your best? What if you don't know what best is?

So when your body rewards your healthy habits with a cancer diagnosis, you feel betrayed. After all, you played by the rules. You said no to treats and you exercised daily, all while surrounded by people who never make time for exercise because they are sitting down eating cinnamon rolls at the mall. You treated your body as a temple while others trashed theirs and yet, you are the one whose life is blown apart by a terrifying diagnosis. It's not fair. You feel disillusioned because life was not supposed to turn out this way. Not for you.

A + B = C ... Or Does It?

From the time we are old enough to get a word of praise or a smiley face on a chart, we operate under the belief that if we make good choices, good things will happen, and if we make bad choices, we're done for. A plus B equals C. The element of truth contained in this belief can be the driving force behind much of our orphan thinking. After all, throughout the Bible we're shown how behavior—good and bad—has consequences, and we're told we will be held accountable for our choices. This truth can provide a healthy motivation for obedient, wise living. The problem arises when we place our hope in a formula of behavior and outcome, choices and results. We think if we do the right thing, we deserve good things to happen to us, and if we mess up, we've missed out on God's best, and we'll never recover. We're on Plan B.

A-plus-B-equals-C thinking is hard to let go of. It is the belief behind statements we hear and make every single day:

"Thank goodness that child has a mother like her. She has advocated nonstop to get him the help he needs with his disabilities. Now he's headed to college!"

"My husband never led our family spiritually, and that's why our children are not walking with the Lord."

"I intend to be debt-free by retirement so I'll have plenty of time and money to enjoy my golden years."

"Everyone told me not to marry him, but I did it anyway. I'll pay for that decision for the rest of my life."

There is absolutely no question that our choices have significant impact, both positive and negative, on our lives and the lives of others. Good choices can lead to good outcomes, and alternatively when we make choices we know to be disobedient, there will probably be natural consequences of those choices, and we are called to repent. However, the redemption story God writes cannot be rewritten by our choices. We will be held accountable for our choices, yes, but God is bigger than our choices, so they cannot trump God's overarching plan. Isaiah 46:9–10 clearly illustrates God's sovereignty over our stories:

Remember the former things, those of long ago;
I am God, and there is no other;
I am God, and there is none like me.
I make known the end from the beginning,
from ancient times, what is still to come.
I say, "My purpose will stand,
and I will do all that I please."

The Burden of a Theology of Good Choices

It is vital to really think through these truths and consider whether or not we actually live as if we believe them. Think about Romans 8:28. It's one of those "feel-good verses." It may hang cross-stitched and framed over your mantle or scrawled on a sticky note on your bathroom mirror. You may nod your head in agreement as you recite, "And we know that in all things God works for the good of those who love him, who have been called according to his purpose." But if we're honest, a more accurate version that has infiltrated so many hearts, minds, and pulpits is this: "And we know that for those who are faithful and diligent to do as they have been taught, all things will work out pretty closely to their pictures of what is good for them and those they love." Or put more simply: "I do my best, and then Jesus does the rest."

But what if you don't do your best? What if you don't know what best is? What if you thought you were doing what was best but you were wrong? What if you did your best but people or circumstances messed it up? Or what if you knew perfectly well what was best and then chose not to do it? *What then?*

Think right now of a decision you made or one someone else made that affected you, or consider an event you feel altered the course of your life and pushed your reality far from the picture you desired. As you imagine the scene in your head, where is the God of the verses above? Where is He? Is He standing off to the side of the scene, watching and wringing His hands with helpless concern? Or does He have His arms crossed, a look of disgust on His face?

Is He nowhere at all?

This exercise may feel uncomfortable. I know life can be cruel, and the memories that just popped into your head may be terribly dark and painful. They may dredge up shame, bitterness, or confusion. It's not easy to think about things you would rather forget. My intention in asking the questions above is to get you out of your head knowledge and help you see more clearly the way you actually view God.

To take Christ's yoke is to believe that no matter what circumstance we find ourselves in, and no matter how we got there, we remain in His picture of what is good for us.

As you think through these questions, what is happening in your body? Is your stomach tightening? Has your pulse quickened? Is your mind beginning to race? Pay close attention to these sensations because your body is trying to tell you what your heart does not want to admit. This is what it feels like to operate under the old yoke.

Though your mind says, "God is in control, and He knows what is best," your anxiety, racing thoughts, and frantic attempt to align life with the picture in your mind reflect a different theology altogether. "I have to get this right, or I'll never attain what is best. I'll be stuck on Plan B . . . or worse."

If it is all up to you, I don't blame you for not sleeping at night. I don't blame you for pushing yourself and everyone around you so hard. If it's all up to you, God must be on the sidelines instead of next to you in the yoke. He must have His clipboard in hand, yelling, "Make Me proud—the family name is at stake," as He watches your performance with scrutinizing eyes. If it is all up to you to get it right, you cannot possibly rest. Too much is at stake.

Life under the weight of the theology of good choices is spiritually crippling. We think we can only feel His presence when life is moving closer to our picture. We only acknowledge He has answered our prayers when He gives us what we think we must have. Consequentially, if we are far from our desired picture, then someone got it wrong, either Him or us. We blame Him for not answering, or we shame ourselves for not doing what we should have done so that He would answer. We tumble through this cycle of shame and blame, shame and blame, our hearts increasing in bitterness with each rotation.

Gerald May, in his book *Addiction and Grace*, says:

> *In our society, we have come to believe that discomfort always means something is wrong. We are conditioned to believe that feelings of distress, pain, deprivation, yearning, and longing mean something is wrong with the way we are living our lives. Conversely, we are convicted that a rightly lived life give us serenity, completion, and fulfillment. Comfort means "right" and distress means "wrong." The influence of such convictions is stifling to the human spirit.*

When we repent of this false theology of good choices, we move from our orphan mentality and behavior to come under the yoke of Christ. "Take it," He offers. He is handing us rest—real rest—but receiving it requires us to release our tight grip on our picture and surrender to His larger picture. To take Christ's yoke is to believe that no matter what circumstance we find ourselves in, and no matter how we got there, we remain in *His* picture of what is good for us. He defines good not by our picture but by His. He promises His presence with us as He works His purposes in our lives—and those purposes cannot be thwarted.

Coming under the yoke of Christ begins with a change of focus. When life takes a turn away from what we desire, our response should shift from "What do *I* do now?" to "What are *You* doing now, and what is my role in *Your* purposes?" The responsibility to make life work is no longer on our shoulders; instead, we are invited to play a role in what He is doing.

The Confusion of Role and Responsibility

So much of our anxiety in life can be relieved if we have a clear understanding of the difference between role and responsibility.

ROLE: *My part in a desired outcome that cannot be achieved without the cooperation of another person and/or circumstance.*

RESPONSIBILITY: *My part in a desired outcome over which I have complete control.*

I see countless well-meaning yet frantic couples in my office who have confused role and responsibility. They assume their responsibility as parents is to ensure their children become successful adults. Of course, their definition of successful is simply their picture of what they think their children should be as adults. This picture usually includes saving faith, a worthy occupation, marriage to a wonderful partner, and lots of grandkids. There's nothing wrong with that picture. As a matter of fact, it closely resembles my own picture for my children. But can I define this outcome as my responsibility? Only if I have complete control, which I do not. Too many other factors are at play.

Like so many of my clients, I will readily tell you I know beyond a shadow of a doubt that I do not have control over my children's lives. And yet, when my picture for my children is threatened, I can demonstrate some crazy behavior suggesting otherwise. When my son missed basketball tryouts because I lost the sign-up sheet or when my daughter had to have her earring surgically removed because I failed to make sure she was following post-piercing protocol, my confusion over role and responsibility sent me to the depths of despair. I believed my son would never find his place in his new school because he wouldn't be on the team, and I assumed my daughter would have an irrational fear of earrings for the rest of

My actions could not have rewritten God's story . . . I'm not that important. None of us is.

her life. And guess what? It would be all my fault . . . or so I thought.

If those predictions had come true (they didn't), it would be absolutely correct to say I had a role in those outcomes. However, they could not have come true without the influence of certain circumstances and actions that were beyond my control. I would have had a role in those outcomes, but they would not have been my responsibility. I would have needed to confess my negligence and ask God to strengthen the areas in which my parenting and organizational skills were weak, but my actions could not have rewritten God's story for their lives. I'm not that important. None of us is.

This was a lesson I had to learn on a much larger scale during a particularly dark time in my life, a season in which my faith could have been destroyed if I had not come to grips with the difference between role and responsibility. It was fall 2012, and I was enjoying a life that was pretty close to my picture. My counseling partner and I had just opened a counseling ministry. I was in the middle of teaching a Bible study that was being filmed for nationwide distribution. My son had graduated from college and was pursuing his career in California. My husband loved his job. My daughters were doing well in school. Everything was on track.

Then one day, out of the blue, reality took a sharp detour further away from my picture than I had ever experienced.

It began with a phone call from my son. He had noticed a lump growing under his arm and decided to get it checked out. He called to say his doctor was sending him for an immediate ultrasound. My world started to tilt. My picture started to shake. Two days and many tests later, my picture was shattered completely with his diagnosis of B-cell non-Hodgkin lymphoma.

Our family was thrust into a world of huge decisions and a new cancer language we neither spoke nor understood. A well-meaning friend who was a cancer survivor said, "You have to get him treated at Cedars-Sinai Medical Center. They have the cutting-edge technology he needs." This would have been good advice if his insurance had been accepted at Cedars-Sinai, but it wasn't; only the smaller hospital nearby would cover his treatment. Fueled by my belief that my son's treatment would determine his outcome, the voices in my head were deafening: "A good mother would do whatever she had to do to secure the absolute best care for her child. Mortgage her house. Sell her hair. Sell her blood. Whatever it takes."

Somehow, in the fog of cancer war, saving my son's life became my responsibility.

We consulted with two oncologists who both confirmed my son's treatment was standard, and he would get the same treatment no matter which hospital he went to. We arranged for him to be treated at the smaller hospital that took his insurance. The night before my son was scheduled to begin chemo, he got a phone call from his doctor.

"Listen, I didn't feel completely comfortable with your pathology report, so I sent your scans to a lymphoma specialist. You don't actually have lymphoma B. This doctor confirmed you actually have Burkitt's lymphoma, a cancer so rare and dangerous that we can't treat you here. We need to completely change your treatment plan and send you to Cedars-Sinai."

Had this error not been caught, my son's cancer would have responded to the original treatment very quickly because that is what Burkitt's does. However, it probably would have returned with a vengeance in his brain and spine. My son's prognosis would not have been good.

God does not ask us to be happy with life outside our pictures; that's not what faith is about.

Would that have been my responsibility? After all, I didn't listen to my friend, the cancer survivor. I didn't research enough to know about the lymphoma expert to whom his doctor sent the report. When my son's original diagnosis and treatment plan were presented to us, I did not demand that the doctor run the lab work again. I didn't read any books by cancer survivors. Some might say I had failed. And yet, God spared him. Did I have a *role* in my son's health? Yes. I had a role in securing the best care for him. But it was God's responsibility to give him what he needed, and His best for my son at that time was to direct him to the treatment that would save his life.

I know what you're thinking. *This story is conveniently easy to tell because your son is still alive.*

You're right. And I'm grateful. But had I lost my son that year, I would tell you today that neither my son's life nor his death was my responsibility because that is a burden God never intended for anyone to bear. To carry a load only meant for the Father would most certainly crush me. Instead, I would pray for faith to cling to the truth that the Father always gives us what we need, whether in life or in death.

I realize how hard this is to hear. It's hard for me to say. I have shared this story in front of a woman whose husband had the same treatment as my son, but her husband died. I do not pretend to understand why. *I don't know why.* It's not OK, and pat assurances that "it will all work out in the end because we know who is on the throne" fall flat for people who are in great pain. Sometimes I scream at the Father because suffering is horrible, and I don't know why some are spared and some are not. God does not ask us to be happy with life outside our pictures; that's not what faith is about. Faith strains to see His face. Faith screams and claws and fights its way to the surface, demanding, "You say You're good. Show me! Open my eyes so I can see You in this dark place."

My son's chemo took him to the brink of death. His face was bloated; his skin was gray. He had no hair, and he had to fight just to breathe. This child I birthed became unrecognizable to me. To add insult to injury, he lost his job, with no prospects in sight, because you can imagine how hirable a cancer patient is.

I remember leaving the hospital and sitting in my hotel room. I was still reeling from my son's grave appearance. I was terrified he wouldn't find another job and would have to pay for his treatment out of pocket. In the weakest voice I whispered, "Where are You? Show me Your presence, God. What are You doing here? *Show me.*"

He Is in This, and He Is in Me

In that frail moment, I put on new glasses with the two crucial lenses that are the foundation of Christ's easy and light yoke: He is in this, and He is in me.

First, He is in this. My son's sickness. The loss of his job. Sin and sickness do not thwart the plan of God. He is here, and His purposes will prevail. And secondly, He is in me. "His divine power has given us everything we need for a godly life" (2 Peter 1:3). This means God has fully equipped me for whatever comes into my life, even my son's cancer.

I wanted to scream, "You've given me *everything* I need? Are you sure, God? Because I'm pretty sure I was standing in the Diet Coke line the day You handed out the maturity gene. I'm mouthy and high maintenance, and I do not do crisis well."

Yet, in a silent California hotel room, broken by my son's brokenness, I had all I needed.

Can you put those glasses on? I know you don't want to. I know it's scary. It may take a sheer act of will in the midst of your pain and confusion, but set those glasses on top of your nose, and hold them in place because they tend to fall off easily. When your picture starts to shake, when you look at the mess you have made of things, when the brokenness of the world touches your life with searing pain, fight to keep those lenses in place. He is in this, and He is in me. If I had not been able to wear those glasses as I stared my son's potential death in the face, I don't think I would have survived it.

I am sorry to say the glasses don't fix everything. Wearing the glasses won't change your circumstances, and they won't ensure you will be happy about whatever adversity you're facing. But they allow you to view life from God's perspective. We serve a powerful and sovereign God who only acts for our good and His glory, and when we believe He is in this—whatever *this* may be—it causes us to look hard for Him when we probably would not have otherwise. We see glimpses of His kindness and commitment to our holiness; we see ways He is changing us for the better. Wearing the glasses makes us free-er. Free-ish. And if you have ever been in great pain, you know that being free-ish, even for a few minutes at a time, is a lifeline. Manna for the moment. In that small moment, choosing to trust in the character of the God who never changes is enough to get you to the next moment.

He is in this; He is in me.

If God can enable a woman like me, who always believed the lie that she was too immature to face a crisis, to put on those glasses as I walked through the worst season of my life, then He can do it for you too. No matter how dark your own season is. And if you're not facing a significant crisis right now? Use the smaller irritations of life to engage with God over what you really believe about Him, and practice making that very conscious choice to pick up those glasses and put them on.

Your kid didn't make the team? He is in this; He is in me.

Your husband arrived home late from work three nights in a row? He is in this; He is in me.

God's greater picture remains.

You didn't get the promotion? He is in this; He is in me.

When you blow it with your kids again, when you think you're making the right decision and it backfires, when you're tempted to believe there is no way God can redeem the mess you've made out of life: He is in this; He is in me.

Practice over and over again the discipline of surrendering your smaller pictures to God's greater picture through the lenses of "He is in this; He is in me." Choose through the small annoyances and the immense tragedies of life to believe that inside or outside of your picture of how you think life should go, God's greater picture remains. No good or bad choices of ours, and no good or bad choices of others, can ever change that. We are His, and He is for us. End of story. Does that make you feel free-er? Free-ish? That is what it feels like to take on Christ's light and easy yoke. Put it on again and again, moment by moment. One time is not enough, because we so quickly forget.

He is in this and He is in me, whether or not A plus B equals C. No circumstance or person can ever change that, praise God.

Process Questions

1. Describe the theology of good choices.

_____

_____

_____

_____

2. How do you see this theology playing out in your life when you get your picture? How about when you don't get your picture?

_____

_____

_____

_____

3. Is there an area in your life where you feel as though you've blown it and you are now on Plan B?

_____

_____

_____

_____

4. In the examples you gave for questions two and three, what did you believe about God that caused you to buy into the false theology of good choices? Spend some time repenting of these assumptions, and repent of your unbelief in the gospel.

_____

_____

_____

_____

5. Meditate on Romans 8:28–29. How does God define what is good for you? Is it you getting your picture, or is it something bigger than that? Pay attention to how your answer makes you feel (anxious, fearful, hopeful, confused, etc.). Take those feelings to the Lord, and ask Him to help you believe and rest in His promise to work all things for your good, as He defines good.

_____

_____

_____

_____

6. In what area of your life do you especially need help believing that "He is in this, and He is in me?" Ask God to help you view your circumstances through these lenses.

_____

_____

_____

_____

Chapter 5

Incompetent and Unashamed

Step 3: Learn from Him (part one)

My husband and I were enjoying a picnic on the shore when we were interrupted by the terrified shouts of a woman swimming in the lake. Apparently she had gone out too deep and was beginning to sink. Several of her family members were swimming close by, but either they weren't paying attention or they weren't taking her seriously, because they weren't responding to her cries. My husband dove in the water and swam toward her. As he struggled to pull her to safety, he quickly learned an important lesson about swimmers in distress. Drowning people are panicked people; they are likely to pull you down with them. This woman had a stranglehold around my husband's neck and was frantically climbing up on his shoulders and head, making it all but impossible for him to swim. She rode like this all the way to the shore. Once they arrived on land, she scrambled off him as fast as she could. Did she fall at his feet in thanks? Offer to buy us dinner? Nope. Without a word to my husband—without even looking at him—she stormed angrily over to her family who had been no help in her crisis, and boy, did she let them have it. They had failed her, and they were going to pay. She couldn't express gratitude to my husband because she was embarrassed. Maybe she was ashamed she almost drowned, or maybe it had more to do with the fact that she had to be rescued by a complete stranger. Shame has to go somewhere, and it can quickly turn to blame. Her family caught the brunt of her blame. "Why didn't you help me?"

I must admit, I often have a similar response when God has to rescue me. I feel ashamed I need His help for the same issue that has tripped me up again and again. I'm irritated when He provides help in a different way from what I had pictured. I have taken my shame out on others who, I feel, should have been there for me. The shame I experience when God rescues me comes from a core belief that I should not need so much help for so long. This belief is a lie—a complete contradiction of the gospel. And yet, I keep believing it.

The invitation to learn from Jesus should be a relief, but frankly it can be a real pride buster. It's tempting to think, *Why haven't I gotten this by now? Why am I still as needy as I was when I first trusted Christ and came under His yoke? Isn't learning all about gaining competence so you don't have to keep asking for help?* Apparently not. In his first letter to the Corinthians, Paul referred to himself as the "least of the apostles" (1 Corinthians 15:9). About a decade later, he identified himself as the "worst" of all sinners (see 1 Timothy 1:15). Rather than demonstrating the upward mobility of performance and position we might expect, Paul descended from the worst of the best to the worst of the worst. But this realization did not lead to shame. Instead, Paul learned to glory in his weakness:

But he said to me,

"My grace is sufficient for you,

for my power is made perfect in weakness."

Therefore I will boast all the more gladly

about my weaknesses,

so that Christ's power may rest on me.

That is why, for Christ's sake,

I delight in weaknesses, in insults, in hardships,

in persecutions, in difficulties.

For when I am weak, then I am strong.

—2 Corinthians 12:9–10

Author and pastor Tim Keller says:

> The more accepted and loved in the gospel we feel, the more and
> more often we will be repenting. And though of course there is
> always some bitterness in any repentance, in the gospel there is
> ultimately sweetness. This creates a radical new dynamic for per-
> sonal growth. The more you see your own flaws and sins, the more
> precious, electrifying, and amazing God's grace appears to you.
> But on the other hand, the more aware you are of God's grace and
> acceptance in Christ, the more able you are to drop your denials and
> self-defenses and admit the true dimensions of your sin.

The closer we are to Christ, the more we see the gap between
where we are and where we are called to be. Paul understood that
despite his years of learning from Christ, he remained incompetent.

We were not designed to achieve a mastery that results in independence.

If you are incompetent, then you have failed to gain mastery over something—you continue to need constant direction, guidance, and instruction. We were not designed to achieve a mastery that results in independence. Christ does not work under the yoke with us until we "get it." Instead, He plows this field called life right alongside us, always, because we will never outgrow our need for Him. In Him, we can be incompetent and unashamed.

When we come under the yoke of Christ, we need His help as we exchange our reactionary, self-focused question, "What do I do now?" for the eternally minded, curious question, "What are You doing now?" Stability—*rest*—are only found when our ears are tuned and our eyes are fixed on the Shepherd. We need Him to teach us how to do that, and in order for us to learn from Him, we have to trust Him.

Christ Is Trustworthy

Our level of trust in God is linked to what we believe about His character. What do we believe about His goodness? How do we think He uses His power and position? Is He really trustworthy, especially with those tender places in our hearts? We must trust our teacher in order to submit to what He says. However, the word *submit* can trigger much apprehension. If we've had power and authority used against us, and most of us have to varying degrees, we may resist vulnerability because we don't want to be harmed again. You may have been raised by a parent who lorded their authority over you with a do-it-or-else approach. Perhaps a boss took advantage of your work ethic. Maybe a spiritual leader let you down in a major way. Maybe you suffered abuse by the hand that was supposed to protect you. Whatever your story, Jesus knows it from beginning to end. He knows all about the resulting fears that can block trust. He kindly addresses those fears by not only inviting us to learn from Him but also by reminding us of who He is . . . the One who is "gentle and humble in heart" (Matthew 11:29).

To be gentle and humble is to lay aside all authority and power with the intent to serve. These characteristics are difficult for me to understand because *gentle* and *humble* are not words I would use to describe myself, especially when I am in a position of authority. I want the job done, and I want it done right. I lose sight of the one doing the job and become easily frustrated when they require more of my time and attention than I feel they should. Not so with Jesus, who "though he was in the form of God, did not count equality with God a thing to be grasped, but emptied himself, taking the form of a servant" (Philippians 2:6–7 ESV). Jesus is the perfect servant leader.

My daughter-in-law is an event coordinator for a Southern California resort. The beachside location and posh reputation make it a highly sought after venue for the extremely privileged. Her clients are well accustomed to superb service, and they are willing to pay plenty for it. A mother once booked the resort for her daughter's wedding, even though her daughter wasn't even engaged yet. The deposit was slightly less than the amount my husband and I paid for our first home. Needless to say, my daughter-in-law's clientele are in a social class far different from my own.

In preparation for one such extravagant wedding, the resort staff was putting the finishing touches on the reception ballroom. Dozens of crisp, white, linen-covered tables were set with china and crystal. Towering exotic floral arrangements were carefully placed on each table. Everything was perfect, ready to go, and the staff opened the doors to let in a gentle sea breeze. Unfortunately, the light wind was more like a gusting gale, knocking over every single centerpiece on every single table. Glass, water, leaves, and petals were everywhere.

Everyone jumped into action, grabbing towels, vases, and brooms. In the midst of the chaos, my daughter-in-law noticed a man in blue jeans and a ball cap working harder than anyone else. She didn't recognize him—was he the florist's assistant? It didn't really matter, because they needed all the help they could get. Miraculously, the tables were cleaned up and reset in time. When the moment arrived for the bridal party to enter the reception and be presented to the guests, she was shocked to recognize the man she assumed to be the floral assistant. Dressed in a tuxedo instead of jeans, he was introduced as the father of the bride.

When my daughter-in-law thought that man was a floral assistant going beyond the call of duty, she was appreciative. But when she learned who he really was, that feeling changed. She knew he could have used his position as a high paying customer to accuse the staff of ineptitude and demand a portion of his money back. Instead, he set aside his position and authority to serve the very staff he had hired to serve him. Understanding who he was and how he used his power completely changed her view of this man. She was no longer simply appreciative. She was stunned with gratitude.

In a similar way, when we remember who Jesus is—the Son of God who gently laid aside His position to love and to serve—and when we recognize the humble way in which He uses His power and authority, any fears we have about trusting Him are replaced with amazement. This amazement pushes us into a place of gratitude, and we are then ready to learn.

Our Skewed View of God's Authority

How do you view God as your authority? How do you relate to Him as your teacher? The answer to these questions is best seen when you mess up again. And again. And again. How do you view Him right after you did that stupid thing again? When you lost your temper again? When you snapped at the kids again? When you looked at that website again? When you chose entertainment over time with Him again? How do you view Him then? Do you see Him as a gentle,

There is no shame in His rescue.

humble servant for whom you are grateful, or do you see Him as that coach we talked about in chapter four, watching from the sidelines, clipboard in hand, vigorously taking notes and shaking His head in disapproval? Do you see Him wringing His hands, stricken and helpless? "Oh my, there she goes again. Straight for the ditch. What am I going to do with her? I've tried to help her, but I'm all out of ideas." Or is He frustrated and angry, rolling His eyes? "Did she seriously just do that *again?* I'm going to have to get back beside her in that yoke and show her—*again.* When is she going to get her act together?"

We often see ourselves and our lousy performance as a nuisance. We think we're bothering Him. We see Him as a dad bent over his desk, typing furiously, snapping, "What do you need this time?" to the child pulling at His sleeve.

How do you really view God when you fail? Don't let what you know you should say get in the way of answering this question honestly. I know you have been taught that God loves you no matter what, but why do you experience so much shame? Why do you cover up your failures? Why do you avoid His gaze when you mess up again?

One consequence of sin is that we now have a predisposition to forget the gospel. We have to be reminded, over and over, that when He saved us, He did not merely get us out of a bad spot with the intention of abandoning us once we reach the point that we really should know better. We have to be told and retold that Jesus actually left His throne in Heaven to rescue us—over and over and over—until He brings us home. There is no shame in His rescue— it's actually a beautiful thing.

The cost of rescue is pride and self-sufficiency. But when we surrender our pride and our plans and look Him in the face, we see how truly loved we are.

Surprised by Love

Consider this psalm written by King David:

But me He caught—
reached all the way from sky to sea;
he pulled me out of that ocean of hate,
that enemy chaos,
the void in which I was drowning.
They hit me when I was down,
but GOD stuck by me.
He stood me up on a wide-open field;
I stood there saved—surprised to be loved!

—Psalm 18:16–19 The Message

David was not rescued when his previous performance declared him worthy of another chance. He was not rescued in order to accomplish great things as a king. He was rescued because he was loved. He was able to experience that love because, unlike the woman my husband rescued from drowning, he did not allow shame to prevent him from looking his Rescuer full in the face. And when he looked Him in the face, he didn't see the anger and disgust his actions may have warranted; he saw love. What a wonderful surprise.

Have you ever been surprised by the Father's love? Not at the moment of your best performance but in your very worst moment, at the point of rescue? If not, then maybe you have been too ashamed to look Him in the face. Lift your head, and look at your Savior's eyes—you'll find no condemnation there.

David continued:

> GOD *made my life complete*
> *when I placed all the pieces before him.*
> *When I got my act together,*
> *he gave me a fresh start.*
> *Now I'm alert to* GOD'*s ways;*
> *I don't take* GOD *for granted.*
> *Every day I review the ways he works;*
> *I try not to miss a trick. I feel put back together,*
> *and I'm watching my step.*
> GOD *rewrote the text of my life when*
> *I opened the book of my heart to his eyes.*
>
> —Psalm 18:20–24 The Message

Once David experienced gratitude, he opened his life to the Father's constant direction. He was hungry to learn so that he could obey the One to whom he was indebted. It is gratitude, not fear, that fuels our desire to learn from Christ.

Gratitude Prepares Our Hearts to Learn

I once had this truth illustrated for me in a little encounter with a highway patrolman. I was late for an out-of-town wedding. Even though I know what a social faux pas it is to enter the chapel on the heels of the wedding party, I was determined not to get a speeding ticket. I traveled through several speed traps, watching my speedometer like a hawk. I was on my absolute best driving behavior, and I arrived at the wedding unscathed by radar guns and blue lights. On the way home, however, I was slightly less intentional. As I chatted away with a friend, my car somehow, someway, sailed right through a red light. Wouldn't you know it? Blue lights. Immediately. But I had been such a good girl! I had tried so hard! I succumbed to just one moment of distraction, and now I was going to pay for it.

I rolled down my window, license and registration ready to hand over to the officer, as he leaned in my window.

"Caught ya" he said.

I nodded sheepishly. "Yeah, you did."

He didn't even take my papers. Instead, he patted me on the arm, cautioned, "Don't let it happen again," and walked away.

I was speechless. He didn't give me what I deserved. He gave me mercy. With renewed intention, I drove home exactly as I had driven to the wedding—carefully and lawfully. But now my obedience had a completely different motivation. I was so thankful for the policeman's mercy that, even though I knew it was really weird, I actually wanted to make him proud of me! I was far out of his sight, (hopefully) never to meet him again, but I heeded his warning and happily stayed well within the speed limit the whole way home.

Mercy overwhelmed me; therefore, gratitude fueled my obedience.

Do you know the One who is asking you to trust Him? Do you understand the character of the One who says, "Learn from Me"? Jesus is gentle and lowly in heart. He has lavished His mercy on you. You don't have to muster up a fear-based obedience, scared of what He will do if you mess up. He does not tire of your need for rescue. *This is why He came.* Christ did not die so you could become a better version of yourself; He died so you could have new life—a life completely dependent upon Him. And He is trustworthy.

Mercy overwhelmed me; therefore, gratitude fueled my obedience.

If you want to learn from Jesus, the cost is your pride—your pride that says you shouldn't have to be rescued again. Your pride that says you shouldn't have to be rescued in a certain way. Your pride that says you should know what to do by now and doesn't want to admit that you don't. Your pride that doesn't want to tug on your busy Father's shirtsleeve again, even though your heavenly Father is nothing like *that* father.

Lay down your pride. Watch as He wades out into that deep place you have gotten into again. Surrender to His offer to carry you back to shore. And when He does, before you scamper out of His arms, look Him square in the face and truly see who has rescued you—not someone who will harm you by using His power against you, but the One who is meek and lowly. The One who left His authority to serve and to rescue you and me.

I pray that when you see His face—when you truly see Him for who He is, in the fullness of His mercy and grace—you will be overcome with gratitude and that gratitude will propel you toward a lifetime of learning from Him.

Process Questions

1. We can't learn from someone we don't trust. How have your past experiences with people in power affected your response to the invitation to surrender to Christ, to come under His yoke?

_____

_____

_____

_____

2. How does Jesus describe Himself in Matthew 11:29? How can His character and the way He uses His power encourage you to trust Him?

_____

_____

_____

_____

3. How do you feel when you find yourself in need of Christ's rescue? Ashamed? Frustrated? Relieved? Thankful? Do you find it hard to look in your Savior's eyes? Why?

_____

_____

_____

_____

4. In what areas of your life do you feel particularly in need of rescue today?

_____

_____

_____

_____

5. Meditate on Psalm 18:27–29. Who does God save? What is the prerequisite for the strength described in verse 29?

_____

_____

_____

_____

6. As you walk through this next week, ask God to show you when you are obeying your picture instead of Him. In those moments, instead of feeling shame, repent and then praise Him for His rescue.

_____

_____

_____

_____

Chapter 6

Hearing Jesus above the Roar of the Train

Step 3: Learn from Him (part two)

A few years ago, I was about to start a new teaching series that was going to be videoed for professional distribution. A trendy friend offered to style me, bless her heart. She saw a glaring need and graciously stepped in and offered her services. No shame here; her observations of my fashion deficiencies were spot on.

Shopping day arrived, and she drove me to a posh designer boutique with upscale clothing. When we entered the shop, my friend did something so strange I couldn't even comprehend it. Instead of beelining straight to the clearance rack like I normally do in any store, she hunted through the full-priced clothing section, picking and choosing without regard to the price tag. What? I didn't even know you could do that! I had no idea you could buy clothing that ended in something besides .99! I thought full-price, in-season clothing was just there in a holding pattern, waiting to be moved to the sales rack. You really can buy that stuff, PRE-discount? I was floored.

She handed me a skirt that, no lie, cost more than my wedding dress. Now, to put things in perspective, my wedding dress cost

$125, but still. I had never, ever paid that much for a skirt, but I took it from her without argument. She then handed me a ridiculously expensive jacket. I said, "Yes, ma'am," and headed straight to the dressing room.

How could I accept these options from her without question? After all, this could have been the perfect opportunity for me to deliver a stirring monologue on the importance of stewardship. I could have argued my points of view on what looks best on me and how much I should be willing to spend. But I didn't because she was the expert. She was a pro in an area I was completely incompetent in, so I wanted to learn all I could from her. And you know what? She knew what she was doing. As she steered me away from flashy patterns and toward classic, quality pieces, I saw the difference in my appearance. The lines of the jacket fell just right; the colors were soft and flattering. Her choices were perfect. I was able to enjoy the gift of this woman's time and expertise because I was incompetent and unashamed. I knew I needed help, and I wasn't ashamed of the fact I needed help. So I was free to learn from her, the expert. I wanted to spend as much time as possible with her because she knew what she was doing.

Hopefully you're at the point now where you honestly desire to learn from the Father. You have seen your need, and you believe Him when He says He is trustworthy. In a sense, you're like me getting ready for that shopping trip. You've got your keys in your hand, you're standing at the door, and you're ready for Him to take you exactly where you need to go.

What's the next step? How do we learn from Him?

We spend time with Him in His Word and in prayer. It's as simple as that.

Psalm 37:4 says, "Delight yourself in the LORD, and he will give you the desires of your heart" (ESV). It would be easy to incorrectly interpret this verse as, "OK, my desire is a job/husband/baby/promotion, so if I enjoy God, He will give me what I want." But if you look at the actual meaning of this Scripture passage, you'll see that is not what it is saying at all. The word *delight*, as it is used here, means, "to be molded by." As we commune with Him, we vulnerably offer our hearts to be shaped by Him. In turn, He shapes our desires to match His.

As we commune with Him, we vulnerably offer our hearts to be shaped by Him. In turn, He shapes our desires to match His.

Think about my style transformation. The more time I spent with my fashionista friend, the more my clothes-buying desires changed to match hers. She didn't just change my look; she altered my thinking and vision. To this day, when I'm shopping I hear her voice in my head saying, "Choose quality over quantity. Classic colors and simple patterns are best. Invest in pieces that will last." Time spent with her, watching and learning and mimicking her ways, changed my desires and shaped my habits. In the same way, the more time I spend with the Father in His Word and in prayer, watching and learning and mimicking His ways, the more my desires, thinking, and vision change to match His.

In his book, *Making All Things New: An Invitation to the Spiritual Life*, Henri Nouwen says:

> *It is clear that we are usually surrounded by so much inner and outer noise that it is hard to truly hear our God when He is speaking to us. We have often become deaf, unable to know when God calls us and unable to understand in which direction He calls us.*

On any given day, who or what do you listen to the most? With whom do you commune the most? The truth is, if you aren't communing with God, then you are most likely communing with your

Communing with God rather than communing with our picture changes and deepens our prayer life because our desires expand beyond our picture and into God's picture.

picture. If you are communing with your picture, then it is your picture, not God, which is shaping you. You may be praying, but you are probably praying over your picture.

"God, heal me."

"God, change her."

"God, let me get the job."

These prayers sound very spiritual. In fact, when your accountability partner asks, "Have you prayed about it?" you can say, "Yes. As a matter of fact, I have."

It's good to entrust God with your desires, but it's important to remember His desires for you may not look exactly like your picture. In fact, they may look nothing like your picture. Your picture can be a good place to start when you approach the Father in prayer, because He cares about your desires, but we need to go deeper. We need to zoom out. Communing with God rather than communing with our picture changes and deepens our prayer life because our desires expand beyond our picture and into God's picture.

It is not our natural inclination to pray this way. Our default response will gravitate toward comfort—always. Our prayers are often a monologue—a one-sided description of our picture. We then end up in despair when we don't get our picture, assuming He hasn't answered.

"He didn't heal me."

"He didn't change her."

"He didn't get me the job."

If I am praying only for my picture, I'm gazing at my picture instead of at Jesus. The Father is absolutely present, working in incredible ways, but I can't see it because I am so focused on my here-and-now circumstances. I then live in despair, falsely accusing Him of not answering, when He has been answering all along. Let me be clear: God answers prayer. Always. But He does not define *answering* as the granting of our pictures, and we are shortsighted to think He does.

In *The Weight of Glory*, C. S. Lewis famously said, "We are far too easily pleased." He's right. I know this because I am not a woman of good appetites in many things. I would always rather have strawberry cake than a salad. I have never uttered the words, "No, thank you. That is too rich for me. Too much fat. I could never eat that much sugar." No. I have always wanted to say those words, but I have never been able to. The truth is, I have bad appetites, and in the beginning of my walk with God, I had bad appetites spiritually too. I knew I should be asking God for the salad—an understanding of His Word and the courage to obey—but what I really wanted was the strawberry cake.

As I have grown and matured in my relationship with God by spending time with Him, my desires have changed and deepened. I still ask for my picture, but at the same time I ask God to help me to long for more. Now I am more likely to pray, "God, this particular circumstance is owning me right now, and it is hard for me to see or ask for anything beyond it. But will you take me deeper?"

Part of sanctification, the process of spiritual growth, is learning how to look beyond our felt needs and ask God to open our eyes to His bigger picture and to cause us to long for His glory, no matter how that plays out. We don't have to be ashamed of the fact we're still rocked by circumstances—that we still want to fight to get our picture—because sanctification is God's responsibility, not ours. Our responsibility is to go to Him and say, "Give me a deeper appetite. Help me to want more. You are in this, and You are in me. Give me an appetite for Your will, regardless of the circumstances." And then we move on that request by faith, despite how we feel.

Hearing from God through His Word

Communing with God must involve dialog. We learn the cadence of our Shepherd's voice by allowing His Word to transform our minds. Scripture provides a grid through which we not only think but also listen to God. When we know what He has already said in Scripture, we can more easily recognize His voice. "My sheep listen to my voice; I know them, and they follow me" (John 10:27).

Being in the Word is essential to learning from Jesus.

May I risk stepping on some toes here? Being in the Word means reading God's Word for yourself, not just reading someone else's thoughts on God's Word. Many of the devotionals we use today allow others to think for us. It is important to remember we no longer need a high priest; we already have One (Hebrews 3:1). We don't need to merely hear how God spoke to someone else; we need Him to speak to us. Are devotionals bad, then? No, but they need to exist only as a supplement to the steady intake of Scripture read by you, meditated on by you.

Get alone with God, just you and His Word, and have what I call a not-so-quiet time. Read, listen, and ask Him to make Himself clear. Wrestle with Him over hard truths and how they apply to hard circumstances.

I have to tell you: Every time you meet with God, you will not have a "hallelujah glory" moment. Dare I say . . . more often than not, your not-so-quiet-time will be more along the lines of taking a daily vitamin. You can't see it working, but you are trusting that it is good for you and is changing you in ways you can't yet see. Do it anyway, because you are desperate for Him. The more time I spend on the front lines in the battle for truth, the more I am aware of my need for Jesus. I'm too scared to speak for Him without spending time with Him. My incompetence—not my polished spirituality—makes me hungry for Him. It makes me show up for my time with Him.

My incompetence— not my polished spirituality—makes me hungry for Him.

When we faithfully take in God's Word, whether we feel like it or not, it changes us. We know this because of two things:

1. **It transforms our thinking (Romans 12:2).**
2. **It shows up in our heads when we need it the most.**

Remember those Bible verses you learned as a kid in Sunday school? My kids still know them, all these years later. Those truths have impacted their lives. And I can think of countless times when I've been in the middle of a tough conversation, decision, or conflict and a verse I meditated on years before is spoken from my lips at just the right moment. When Scripture is stored in our heads and hearts, it acts as a holy arsenal, ready to be retrieved by the Holy Spirit and put into action in all aspects of our lives—from the mundane to the really, really hard. God instructs us through His Word. It is awfully difficult to engage in dialog with Him if we don't have a strong understanding of Scripture.

Afraid to Ask

When I teach about communing with God, I often get pushback from mature believers, like the gentleman who once said to me, "That stuff you talk about—about hearing God—that scares me. Because what if I ask Him and He doesn't say anything? My fear would be

> *God always honors a heart that desires to do His will, and He is bigger than my lack of human ability to always hear Him correctly.*

confirmed—my fear that everybody else is somehow in the club and I'm not. I figure it's better not to ask Him anything than to ask and find out that I'm some kind of stepchild."

Are you also scared to ask Him because you're scared He won't speak? Are you afraid you will look like a fool or, worse, that your faith will be damaged? After all, there are plenty of people who have walked away from the faith because they felt as though their prayers never went further than the ceiling.

Please understand, I am not talking about hearing audible words from God. The conversation I am describing is one in which I ask the Father to speak, I engage with His Word, and then I move tentatively, saying, "To the best of my ability, this is what I believe God is telling me."

I may get it wrong. My feeling of God's leading could actually have something to do with what I ate for lunch that day. But that doesn't keep me from asking, from listening, from trying to obey. Honestly, what is the meaning of a personal relationship with Jesus if we can't ask Him to speak to us? Scripture doesn't directly cover our questions of "Whose house should we go to on Christmas morning?" or "Should my child go to public or private school?" or "Should I take the job?" so we need to ask, and we need to listen. God always honors a heart that desires to do His will, and He is bigger than my lack of human ability to always hear Him correctly.

Our Neediness Requires Us to Come

I have often wondered why the Bible does not specifically address every possible circumstance and every question we may have. But

I think perhaps God did it on purpose so that we would have to come to Him and ask.

When our kids went to college, we rigged their financial situation so that they ran out of money halfway through each month. We only put two weeks' worth of funds in at a time so that they would have to call us to ask for more. The phone rang halfway through each month, like clockwork.

"Hey Mom and Dad! Me again. How are you? Good to hear. I'm fine too. Yeah, so, about my bank account . . ."

How do you think we felt when they called? Used? No. We felt happy. We wanted an ongoing relationship with them. If they didn't need us, if we had completely covered all their needs in advance, then they might have never called. We didn't care why they called us; we just wanted time with them.

God has, in a sense, "rigged" life so we have no choice but to come to Him. He has given us wonderful principles, but He has not given us every specific application to every possible situation. So we need Him. We have to engage with Him, wrestle with Him, read His Word, and listen for the cadence of His voice because the same question asked on two different occasions could require different answers, depending on the circumstances.

"God, my teenager just mouthed off to me and stormed up the stairs. Your Word says to love, but it also says to instruct. What does it look like to love and instruct here, today, in this moment?"

On one day, the answer may be to stand firm and take away privileges. On another day, the answer may be to make her favorite snack and take it to her room. We don't have the wisdom to know for sure, but He does, so we ask. We listen. We tentatively step forward in what seems like obedience, and we trust Him with the outcome.

Our Prayer Posture

As we come to the Father, engaging Him through His Word, our prayer posture—the way in which we come to the Father—is essential. In fact, when Jesus taught the disciples in Matthew 6 how to pray, He started out by addressing their posture.

Prayer	Posture
"This, then, is how you should pray: 'Our Father'" (v. 9).	Childlike, approaching our Father who loves us.
"Hallowed be your name" (v. 9).	You are holy, God. I am in awe of You.
"Your kingdom come, your will be done, on earth as it is in heaven" (v. 10).	Despite what my picture is, despite my opinions on how I want my life to go, what matters above all else is Your will and Your glory.

In teaching them how to pray, Jesus communicated, "The very first thing you must do is to posture your heart as a child who understands your Father loves you and knows what is best." By following Jesus' command and taking on this posture when we spend time with Him, we are not denying our picture; in fact, it's important to acknowledge our picture before Him because He knows our hearts anyway. But the posture Jesus is calling us to allows us to back away—zoom out—from our picture and align our hearts with the bigger picture of His will. In essence, we are saying, "You know what I long for, Father. But I want Your will to be done because I trust You."

Our Core Desire

In teaching us to pray in this way, Jesus appeals to the true core desire that is given to us at the point of salvation. When we are redeemed, God gives us not just grace and mercy but a new heart that contains a new core desire.

I will give you a new heart
and put a new spirit in you;
I will remove from you your heart of stone
and give you a heart of flesh.
And I will put my Spirit in you
and move you to follow my decrees
and be careful to keep my laws.

—Ezekiel 36:26–27

At the point of conversion, God takes out your heart of stone and gives you a new heart. Done. As a Christian, your core desire is to glorify God through your obedience. This may not be what you are living out of; you may still long for your picture, but the desire for God's glory remains at the core of who you are if you are a follower of Jesus.

Sometimes when I read verses like this, it feels as though someone is telling me I'm a size four, natural blonde. I want to say, "I don't think so. Have you seen what I've done lately? Do you think that shows that I really want God's glory? No. I think what I really want is my own picture, and I do things I know are wrong because I'm not getting what I want, and I just don't care anymore." But my behavior does not make these verses untrue because my core desire and

> *My behavior does not make these verses untrue because my core desire and my identity come not from what I do but from what He did.*

my identity come not from what I do but from what He did. Second Corinthians 5:17 says, "Therefore, if anyone is in Christ, he is a new creation; old things have passed away; behold, all things have become new" (NKJV).

Notice this verse reads, "He *is* a new creation," not, "He *will be* a new creation." When we are redeemed, we are made new. It's done.

What would happen if we as the church really believed He makes us completely new at the point of salvation? That we don't have to do anything to earn His favor or love? I know what we wouldn't do. We wouldn't ask less of each other. And we wouldn't pound each other with rules because, really, we know the rules. Instead, we would say to each other, "*Remember.*" We would say, "This is who you are in Him. Did you forget? Oh, and this behavior? This isn't who you really are. You've forgotten your name. You've forgotten whose you are. You are not doing what you deeply desire to do, which is to glorify God." We would then point each other to the Father who says, "Learn from me. I want to teach you what it looks like to follow Me and My ways."

Our families, relationships, and churches would be transformed if we approached each other in this way. We ourselves would be transformed as we remembered His character, trusted Him, and obeyed. In the process of learning from Him, we would begin to own our God-given core desire to glorify Him. We would start to see the things God gives us in light of our core desire. We would hear Jesus say, "Remember—this is what you really want. Not just your picture—not just the healing or the job or the restored relationship. Above all else, you want to glorify Me."

You may be scared to pray, "Your kingdom come, your will be done." I get how these statements are terrifying. Tell that to the Father. "God, this terrifies me to pray this way because You know how desperately I want my picture. Would You please give me an appetite for Your will? I'm scared; would You help me to live in alignment with my deepest desire?"

As you pray in this way, strange things start to happen. Your attitude toward your difficult co-worker softens, and you begin to see her in a different light. Instead of praying, "God, change her!" you shift to, "God, how do You see her? What does love look like here?" When you're wronged, instead of pleading, "God, make this right!" you begin to pray, "Jesus, You know what it feels like to be mocked, misunderstood, and falsely accused. I do long for You to make this right, but in the meantime, would You show me how to honor You as I bear up under injustice?" These Christlike prayers and attitudes come from the Scripture that is stored in your heart.

As you engage with the Father, informed by His Word, praying with a posture of humility and submission, you slowly unhitch from your picture and hitch to the Rock who is unchanging and secure. What He gives you won't necessarily match your picture, but somehow, you feel a kernel of hope beyond what you can see. You can experience deep longing, yet feel completely satisfied, both at the same time. You may be praying for community and are lonelier than you have ever felt in your life, but at the same time, in the waiting, you feel held. Somehow, both of these things can coexist, and in the midst of them you can experience sanity, rest, and peace.

You have a mentor who is an expert in His field. He knows the ropes; in fact, He made the ropes. He is offering to spend as much time with you as you want, free of charge. He is ready to teach you all you need to know about the areas in which you are incompetent—wisdom, discernment, decision-making, obedience, love, trust. If you have a listening ear, He's willing to show you His ways, and He won't get impatient or frustrated if you don't understand and need to ask Him to clarify. He may instruct you to do some things and think about some things in such a way that feels awkward and foreign to you, but because you trust Him—because He not only knows what is best but also loves you with a perfect Father's love—you'll listen. You'll take notes. You'll obey. Your desires will slowly change to match His, and though it may be painful, you'll say, "This is right."

If a human offered you this kind of deal in regard to parenting or marriage or organizational skills or any other area in which you felt deficient, you would sign up in a heartbeat. You know you would. Will you accept this most generous offer from your Father? Show up—He's waiting for you.

Process Questions

1. Think of a specific instance when you defined God answering your prayers as getting what you want, i.e., your picture. How is this definition shortsighted? How can it lead to bitterness and resentment? What does it really look like for God to answer your prayers?

_____

_____

_____

_____

2. Why is it so crucial that we immerse ourselves in God's Word? How does His Word change our desires?

_____

_____

_____

_____

3. Are you scared to ask God to speak to you? Why or why not?

_____

_____

_____

_____

4. Read the following Scripture passages, and ask God to reveal Himself to you. This is His Word to you. What does He want to say to you today through these verses?

PSALM 1:1–3

What word or phrase stands out to you?

_____

_____

_____

_____

How can one flourish and grow spiritually like the tree by the water?

_____

_____

_____

_____

What adjustments in your attitude, practices, or relationships need to happen in order for this kind of spiritual health to take place? Of what do you need to repent?

_____

_____

_____

_____

1 KINGS 19:9–13

Do you ever get frustrated because it seems like other people hear from God but you don't? Why do you think this is?

_____

_____

_____

_____

Why do you think God chose to reveal Himself not in a loud, flashy way, but in a whisper? Consider Jesus' instructions to the disciples on how to come before the Father in prayer. How do you need to better position yourself to hear God's still, small voice?

_____

_____

_____

_____

5. Take your picture before the Father. Name it and own it. Then ask Him to help you zoom out and see your picture in light of the bigger picture of His glory.

_____

_____

_____

_____

Chapter 7

Aligning Your Thinking with Your Theology

Step 3: Learn from Him (part 3)

I am not an excellent driver. I'm not the greatest at paying attention to details, and as you can imagine, this is not the best trait to possess when you are behind the wheel of a car. As a—let's call it, "challenged driver"—I'm thankful for road accommodations to help me out, such as signs that say, "Keep right," clearly marked turn lanes, and driveway entrance ramps.

Driveway entrance ramps, you ask? Oh yes. A more proficient, detail-oriented driver might be able to slowly back out of the garage and across the dip between the driveway and the road without a problem, but I am guaranteed to bottom out every single time. Boom! *Scraaaaape.* Every time. But once that entrance ramp is laid over the dip, I can reverse with confidence, ease, and little to no damage.

As we spend time with Jesus in His Word and in prayer, learning His ways, voice, and direction, we are essentially laying ramps of truth over the ditches of our former way of thinking. We're replacing the worship of our pictures and our orphan mentality—"If it's to be, it's up to me,"—with the gospel truths that our righteousness is found in Christ alone and we are well-provided-for children of the King. Laying down these truths is hard work because we are prone to forget our status as His children and heirs. Our ditches—our mental ruts of old thinking—can be quite deep.

Ephesians 4:22–23 says, "You were taught, with regard to your former way of life, to put off your old self, which is being corrupted by its deceitful desires; to be made new in the attitude of your minds." Our desires become deceitful when we look to them, rather than Christ, for life—when they are actually no longer desires but demands we believe we cannot function without. Yet as sons and daughters, we are no longer slaves to these deceitful desires. Our minds can be made new.

Prior to the latter half of the twentieth century, scientific consensus held that our brains are fully developed in early childhood and remain relatively unchanged throughout our lives. Since then, research has shown our brains can be altered—they are malleable well into adulthood. Renowned neuroscientist Dr. Michael Merzenich says, "Your brain—every brain—is a work in progress. It is 'plastic.' From the day we're born to the day we die, it continuously revises and remodels, improving or slowly declining, as a function of how we use it."

Neuroplasticity is a broad term used to describe the amazing ability the brain has to reorganize itself by forming new neural connections. Nerve cells in the brain are actually capable of compensating for injuries caused by disease or trauma, and they can adjust their activities in response to new situations or changes in a person's environment. For example, the brains of children adopted from institutional settings in which they experienced the trauma of fear, abandonment, and neglect can actually change as the children experience safety, security, and love. Their brains can transform to create new pathways that result in healthier thinking, feeling, and processing. Once again, science has caught up with what Scripture already says: Our minds can be rewired to replace our ruts—well-worn paths that lead us into emotional, spiritual, and physical unhealthiness—with new paths of thinking that enable us to make choices that align with who we really want to be. But it takes work to form new paths.

Good Theology, Bad Thinking

As a counselor, I spend much of my time working with believers who have been exposed to excellent teaching but have little understanding of how to apply what they have been taught. Interestingly, this gap

Solid teaching is of little value if we are not able to align it with the thoughts we consistently allow to play in our heads.

between theology and thinking tends to be widest in the clients who have the most theological training. We can become so sure of what we know that we do not allow ourselves to look at the discrepancies between what we say we believe and what we actually think and live out. Solid teaching is of little value if we are not able to align it with the thoughts we consistently allow to play in our heads.

Second Corinthians 10:5 instructs us to "take captive every thought to make it obedient to Christ." We cannot do this if we don't take a good, hard look at our thoughts.

A helpful technique I like to use with clients to move them past their stated theology and down to their actual thinking is an exercise I call freeze framing. When a client is describing a situation in which he or she lost control and behaved in a way they later regretted, I ask the client to zero in on the moment right before they got to the crazy place. I know the person seated in front of me in my office knows the truth about their identity and provision in Christ because they're now calm and removed enough from the situation to remember the truth. But what about the person who lost it? In those moments right before the poor behavior, what were they thinking? When we want to get to the bottom of why we behave as we do in crisis moments, it is helpful to work backward toward what we are truly allowing ourselves to think and believe.

Ask me in a sane moment what my beliefs are about the sovereignty, power, and love of God and you will probably get a solid, biblical answer. But when I just learned the promotion I wanted went to someone much less qualified, my thinking may be quite different. I am prone to go down the unbelief side of the chart we examined in chapter three and think, *This is so unfair. It doesn't matter how hard I work; it's all about politics. No one has my back here. It's every man for himself.* As you can see, the thoughts I allow to play in my mind during a crisis are considerably different from the ones I know to be true. There is a significant difference between my stated theology and my pragmatic theology. It is essential that I uncover the way I am truly thinking because it is actually my thinking, rather than my circumstances, that fuels my feelings and drives my actions.

Consider this example: Your child comes home from school crying. You say, "What's the matter, sweetheart?" She tells you an event that happened at school: All her friends were invited to a party, but she was left out. According to her account, not being invited to the party made her sad. A negative event produced a negative feeling. But this explanation is not exactly accurate. An event can't create emotions; events lead to thinking, and thinking leads to feelings. Feelings, in turn, lead to actions.

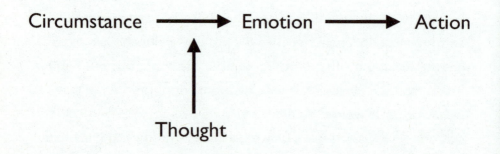

Circumstance ⟶ Emotion ⟶ Action

Thought

The horizontal portion of this chart represents what most of us think as the natural flow of why we feel and behave as we do. But do you see the vertical arrow below the others? That arrow is often missed. We naturally assume circumstances cause us to feel a certain way, and because of the way we feel, we sometimes do certain things we don't really want to do. But the circumstance is not the culprit; the thoughts between the circumstance and the feelings are. That's why two people can respond to the same event in completely different ways. They interpret the event, or think about the event, differently. We don't feel because of what happened; we feel because of what we *think* about what happened. And the way we think about our circumstances is the difference between crazy and rational behavior.

"Above all else, guard your heart, for everything you do flows from it" (Proverbs 4:23). If our feelings lead to our actions, how do we direct our feelings? By guarding our thinking.

The Courtroom of Your Mind

Picture your mind as a courtroom. The members of the jury are your feelings, and the witnesses called to the stand are your thoughts. A jury makes its decision—it acts—based on the evidence it hears from witnesses, so who gets called to the stand is crucial to any case. A witness is inhibited by strict rules. He is bound to not only tell the truth, but to tell the provable truth. He can't share hearsay; he can only share provable facts.

Imagine a courtroom where the judge lifted these rules and witnesses were allowed to say whatever they wanted to say. What chaos! The jury would be subjected to a roller coaster ride of ups, downs, and confusion, and then they would have to make a decision based on everything they heard, provable or not. How scary would that courtroom be? And yet, that is often the scene in our minds when life deviates from our picture. Chaos erupts; the witnesses (our thoughts) start shouting all kinds of false or unprovable information, and our feelings get taken for a crazy ride. We then act out of these unstable feelings, doing things we would never in our right minds do, and later wonder, *How did I get here? I don't even recognize myself. Why did I do that? Why did I say that?*

Let's pause a minute for some clarification. If you think I am under the illusion you are not going to be emotionally impacted by difficult situations, you don't know me very well. I am a feeler. I feel deeply, and I often verge on lunacy. I'm kind of known for it. But there is a difference between being emotional and being driven to despair. There is a difference between feeling deeply and being emotionally out of control and as a result, making really bad choices you will be ashamed of ten minutes later.

Think of emotions as a one to ten scale, one being you on the beach without a care in the world and ten being you in the ultimate crazy place, doing things you are going to soon be embarrassed about. It is possible to be jolted from a one to a seven in an instant, without even doing anything. Your husband calls and in a somber voice says, "Honey, are you sitting down?" Boom! You're at a seven, and there's not much you can do about that. But eight to ten is the crazy place, and it is optional. People and circumstances can knock you out of a happy place into a disrupted place, and that is out of your control. But you can control whether or not you launch into the crazy zone. It is not your fault when you get disrupted; however, you do have the capability to stay out of the crazy zone. Learning to control your thoughts—to take each one captive and make it obedient to Christ—is how you stay out of that eight to ten range. You have to wake up your inner judge and lay down the law in your head.

The deeper you are in difficult circumstances, the more crucial it is for you learn how to bring your thought life into obedience to Christ. Prior to my son's cancer diagnosis, I often lived out of a very misaligned thought life. Being a deep feeler, I was extremely aware of my emotions, but I was not as in touch with what was really driving those emotions. But when your child has cancer, if you don't grab onto your head, you can go to the crazy place and never come out. For me, the stakes were really high. My life—my son's life—was completely out of my control and in the hands of physicians, cancer cells, CT scans, and medications I couldn't pronounce. I had to learn how to protect my thought life or else I wouldn't have been able to keep going. I wouldn't have made it out with my sanity somewhat intact.

Guarding Our Minds

In a practical sense, how do we guard our minds?

1. **Use your feelings as indicators, not dictators.**

   Recently my change oil light came on in my car. I drove to the nearest service station as fast as I could. I told the mechanic, "This light came on. Can you check and see what's going on?" Notice I didn't say, "This light came on. Change my oil." There's a big difference between, "Change the oil," and, "Please check the oil." I asked the mechanic to investigate the situation because the light came on; I didn't demand they acquiesce to what the light was saying. This is exactly how we should use our feelings—as indicator lights. Ask, "What is this feeling telling me to consider?" Don't assume the answer is as obvious as you may think.

2. **Do not shut down your feelings.**

   A car without indicator lights is dangerous. If you turn off that indicator light—if you shut your feelings down—you are in danger of missing some valuable data. Feelings are neither right nor

You're free to explore the why behind the feeling because you know you are treasured by the One who is doing the searching.

wrong; they just are. We can be quick to evaluate feelings as good or bad. They are neither. If we shut them down as wrong or elevate them as justified, we will miss an opportunity to become curious about what they are actually trying to tell us. Feelings are not the point. What if I went to the mechanic and asked, "Could you please change my indicator light? It keeps coming up red and red is bad, so could you change it to blue?" The mechanic would probably shoot me a strange look and say, "Ma'am, it doesn't matter what color your indicator light is; what matters is what the light is trying to tell you."

Paying attention to our feelings can be difficult and painful work, which is why we often avoid looking more deeply into what they reveal. It's why we would rather run away from them, if at all possible. When we numb our feelings or act out of them without examining them we are not allowing Christ to use them to teach us.

For example, you may be talking to your friend about a co-worker and say, "She turned her report in late, again! I'm so angry I want to rip her head off!" And then you feel really embarrassed, so you retract. "Oh my goodness, that was a horrible thing to say, wasn't it? I'm sorry. I didn't mean that." You shut down, silently pray, "Jesus, forgive me for wanting to rip her head off," and move on. But what if instead, because of the freedom you have in the gospel and the trusting, vulnerable relationship you have with the Father, you prayed, "Wow, Jesus. I'm really angry. What's going on?"

Do you see the difference? You're not saying what you felt was right; you are simply owning that feeling and submitting yourself to the process of looking deeper into the thinking and beliefs that expose why you feel as you do. You're free to explore the why behind the feeling because you know you are treasured by the One who is doing the searching. You can reject the enemy's accusation that you should know better and say, "The light is going off, God. Search me. Help me figure out why."

3. Follow the feeling to the thought and make the necessary adjustments.

It's important to determine the thoughts that shoot you from "I'm upset but stable" into the stratospheres of the eight to ten range of "I'm crazy upset." These turbo thoughts catapult you up to the crazy range by taking you from a provable reality to the unprovable.

Detecting your turbo thoughts is a simple process of asking the following four questions when your indicator light comes on (when you experience any strong negative emotion). By way of illustration, as we walk through these four questions, I'm going to use our example of the co-worker who turned in the report late.

- **What was I thinking right before I began to feel this way?**
  Avoid intense introspection at this point, as that kind of soul-searching will only take you deeper into an emotional vortex. Two or three sentences will suffice. "She always does this. She doesn't care at all about how she affects the workload of everyone else. She'll never be a team player."
- **Are these thoughts provable 100 percent of the time?**
  Note that the question is not, "Are these thoughts true?" It is possible a thought may actually be true but is not yet provable. And besides, when you are in great distress, whatever you are thinking in that moment feels absolutely true, so you will probably respond with defensiveness. The question at this point is not, "Is it true?" but "Is it provable 100 percent of the time?"

All of the thoughts you had about your co-worker are unprovable. "She always does this" is not a statement that is provable 100 percent of the time. It may be true some of the time, but it is likely not true all of the time. "She doesn't care about my time" may in fact be true, but it cannot be proven because we do not have the ability to see into another's heart and mind to determine what they feel or think. Finally, "She will never be a team player" is a prediction of the future based upon the present. Again, this may actually turn out to be true, but it is not, at present, provable.

If a trial witness gives a statement that is an opinion or is based on incomplete information, an attorney will likely object as it is conjecture—an unprovable opinion. The statement may actually be true, but the judge will sustain the objection and strike the statement from the record so that the jury cannot use the statement to determine a verdict. The same standard must be used in the courtroom of your mind. The only exception to this rule would be if the witness were an expert—someone with credible and impartial knowledge. We often view ourselves as expert witnesses, especially when it comes to the thoughts and feelings of those we have history with. We can also try to use that history to predict the future, but Scripture is clear. There is only One who is able to discern the hearts and minds of men (Jeremiah 17:9–10) and who knows the future (Psalm 139:16).

Assuming we are expert witnesses is not simply wrong thinking; it is a dangerous placement of ourselves on the same level as God. These are His characteristics and His alone; He did not give them to us. When you are stable in the here and now, you are much better equipped to deal with future crises than when you waste time and energy playing the what-if game.

We must reject the temptation to play God and instead ask ourselves, "Is it provable 100 percent of the time?" The answer is usually no. You may want to kick, scream, and insist, "You don't understand! I know it's true! It's true! It's true! It's true!" It may be true. You can deal

Circumstances and events don't drive our emotional storms; our thinking does.

with that when the time comes, but the only safe place for us to be is in the present. That is all we are responsible for. God says, "Don't go there. That's My job, not yours. It is unnecessarily painful for you to try to go there. I haven't given you the abilities to prophesy or discern another person's head or heart because I love you, and I know you cannot handle them. Don't go there. It's a dangerous place; it is a crazy place. Leave it to Me."

Trust Him, and don't try to do what you were not designed to do.

- **Whenever I think those unprovable thoughts, where do I head emotionally?**

When we allow ourselves to think unprovable thoughts, the emotions that result are intensified, making us feel unstable and out of control. When you believed your co-worker was lazy, didn't care about your time, and would never be a team player, you felt enraged. This is an intense, out-of-control feeling.

It is crucial we make the connection between our thoughts and the feelings that result from our thinking. When we make this connection, we are able to see that we are not the victims of whatever happens to us. This realization is life altering. The plunge down the emotional vortex can be stopped when we understand circumstances and events don't drive our emotional storms; our thinking does.

- **When I feel this way, how do I behave? Is my behavior congruent with what I really want to do?**

When you feel enraged, what do you usually do? I know what I do. I say really foolish things—hurtful things that damage others, words I can't take back. I immediately regret those words.

You felt enraged when you thought unprovable thoughts about your co-worker. So what did you do? You said you wanted to physically harm her. Is that what you really want to do—slander your co-worker and threaten bodily harm? No.

Building New Pathways of Belief

Now that we know the four questions to ask ourselves when our indicator light comes on, what is the solution? "I know I feel enraged because I'm believing these things that are not provable, and I know I made some really poor choices because I felt enraged. So how about this: I'll just stop being angry!" How well does that work for you? Even if you are able to suppress your anger externally, if left unattended, anger has to go somewhere and it usually resurfaces in the form of bitterness.

We need to build new pathways in our minds. This is a simple process but not an easy process.

"The report is late. Again. I feel really angry. My indicator light is on. What is it trying to tell me? What am I really thinking? I'm thinking the report is late, and she is lazy and doesn't care about my time. These thoughts are not working for me because I can only prove one of them, and they are making me feel really out of control. If I choose to dwell on these things, I am no longer in control of my day or my mood; my co-worker is. I need to go down a new path and replace my former thinking with provable thoughts: *The report is late, and I really don't know why.* Period."

Pretty simple, I know. The idea is to state provable facts, as you know them in the here and now. Notice, these are not necessarily positive thoughts that make you feel better. If you were to say, "The report is late, but I'm sure she didn't mean to inconvenience me. It will be OK. I'm sure it won't happen again," your brain would automatically reject that line of thinking. Those thoughts may be positive, but they are also unprovable. Contrary to what our culture may tell us, positive thinking is not the answer. We are not trying to make ourselves feel positive; we are simply trying to stabilize our emotions so we can make behavioral choices more in line with who we really are as children of the King.

Contrary to what our culture may tell us, positive thinking is not the answer. We are not trying to make ourselves feel positive; we are simply trying to stabilize our emotions so we can make behavioral choices more in line with who we really are as children of the King.

How do you feel when you tell yourself those two, provable statements, "The report is late," and, "I don't know why"? Do you feel crazy and out of control? Do you want to hurt somebody? Probably not. Those three little words, "I don't know," help remove yourself from the crazy range and into a zone that's much more manageable. More sane. You still may not be happy about the report being late, but the goal is not to get you to a happy state; the goal is to get you stable. When you are stable, you can behave in a way that is more congruent with what you believe. You are going to have a very different conversation with your co-worker when you are stable than you would have had when you were convinced she didn't turn in the report because she's lazy and doesn't care about you. Again, you may still be upset. That's OK. But your intensity will be much lower. The poison has been taken out of the conversation.

It is crucial to constantly talk to yourself. I know that may feel unusual, but it is vital to your sanity. Deal with the intensity of your feelings by dealing with your thinking. The conversation in your mind might go something like this:

"That thing she did, the thing you're so upset about? You don't know why she did that."

"Yes, I do!"

"No, you don't. Is what you're thinking 100 percent provable?"

Again, if you ask yourself, "Is it true?" you're not going to listen to yourself. The intensity of your emotions will insist, "You'd better believe it's true!" But if you say, "It might be true—she might be lazy—but is it provable 100 percent of the time?" the intensity is sucked out of the situation. Then you can be calm enough to listen and respond.

"I can't prove it. I really don't know why she turned the report in late. God has only given me the grace to deal with what is provable, so in my thoughts and emotions, that's where I have to stay."

Play a New Tape

This exercise is hard work. I get it. My clients tell me all the time, "This is too hard! It takes too much time. I can't do this!" But can I tell you something? You're already doing it. We all play tapes in our heads. We listen to those tapes over and over, and we act on those tapes. All I am asking you to do is to pop in a new tape. The process of playing new tapes repetitively creates a new pathway of thought in your brain. The more you go down that new path, the easier it will be to believe those thoughts, and eventually the path becomes so well worn, your brain automatically goes to it when presented with similar challenges.

As I have asked God to turn up the volume on my thought life so I can take a closer look, I have discovered I only have about ten tapes, and they loop in my head all day long. My tapes relay messages such as, "Everybody's against me," and, "I'm a loser." I have certain tapes for people in my life too. And for God. When you turn up the volume on your thought life and listen—*really listen*—you'll notice your tapes playing on repeat also. "Oh, that's the I'm-only-valuable-when-I-per-form-well tape! I've heard that one before!" And then you can talk yourself toward the truth. "I've heard this tape before, and I don't want to fall for it again. I don't know why that person didn't talk to me after I spoke at the meeting. I don't know why. I just know she didn't speak to me, and more than that, I know my worth does not rest in my per-formance." I just took out the old, unprovable, condemning tape and replaced it with a tape that is 100 percent provable. I'm looping a new tape, and my thoughts and emotions are much more stable.

The Power of "I Don't Know"

"But how can I tell myself I don't know when I really do know? I mean, what if I really do know?"

I get this, because I think I really do know too. I get paid money to read people and know. As my husband likes to say, I am "not always right but always sure." So speaking as much to myself as I am speaking to you, I'm telling you: play the tape anyway. "I don't know why . . . I don't know how . . . I don't know if . . ." Even if you don't believe it, play the tape anyway because simply telling yourself those three words, "I don't know" will lower your intensity and drop you down out of the crazy zone. Only then will you be able to have a calmer conversation with whoever upset you. The outcome will be one of two things: Either your previous suspicions will be confirmed and you will be at a more stable place to deal with them or you will find out you were completely wrong and you'll be more than a little bit humbled. You may find out your co-worker's husband recently abandoned her and her child with special needs. Don't you feel about an inch tall when things like that happen? When you've had all kinds of ugly thoughts about someone only to discover they are in the midst of deep pain? We are not as brilliant as we think we are. Hooking on to this thought alone should help prevent us from jumping to conclusions.

Fifty-some-odd years into life, I can say I'm a little less sure than I once was because I have become an honest believer in the tape that says, "I don't know." I became a believer of that tape by playing it over and over and over and acting on it by faith, even when I didn't believe it was true.

So, your daughter who came home from school sad because everyone was invited to the party except for her? As a mother, I know we often believe it is our job to make our children feel better, but that belief can drive us to make comments that are unprovable and unhelpful—comments like, "Oh, sugar muffin! They probably just lost the invitation. I'm sure you'll get one tomorrow." Or how about this one? "They're just jealous, sweetie, that's all." That may be positive thinking, but it absolutely will not work because as positive as those thoughts may be, they are not provable.

How about a different approach? "Honey, I can understand why you're sad. I'm so sorry. I don't know why they didn't invite you. You don't, either. But you know what? That one party? It does not define who you are."

Do you see how I didn't try to make her happy? That is not my goal. My goal is to empathize, remind her of what is provable, and keep her in the here and now.

"They didn't invite me because everyone hates me!" she says.

"Sweetheart, you can't prove that. All you know is you weren't invited. That is all you know for now."

My daughter was once in a similar situation, and when I asked if her thoughts were provable 100 percent of the time, she said, "Well, 99 percent of the time!" I replied, "Then let's focus on that 1 percent, because when you focus on the 99 percent, you feel miserable. But when you focus on the 1 percent, you may not be happy, but at least you're sane."

Assumptions rob us of relationship.

Oftentimes, when we act on our assumptions, we end up creating a self-fulfilling prophecy. What if my daughter had acted on the 99 percent? "Everyone hates me, so I'll sit by myself and not talk to anyone." Then what would have happened? She would have been all alone, and no one would have talked to her. Would they have not talked to her because they disliked her or because she appeared standoffish? There is no way to know for sure.

Are there ways in which you have created self-fulfilling prophecies in your own life because you acted on your assumptions about others' thoughts and motives? You want community, but no one greeted you at church, so you think no one likes you. Feeling hurt, you pull away, and then guess what? You don't have community.

Assumptions rob us of relationship.

As you focus your thoughts on what is provable, using the pattern, "I don't know [fill in the blank]," over and over again, your mind will literally change. You'll undo the toxic, unprovable ruts and create new, healthy pathways. "I don't know that; I do know this. I can't change that; I can change this." You can take control back from circumstances or people and regain the sanity needed to move forward. Your emotional stability can be handed back to you, thank goodness. Will you still be in great pain? Maybe. But remember: pain cannot be avoided; despair can.

Pain is inevitable; *crazy is optional.*

Process Questions

1. Psalm 139:23–24 says, "Search me, God, and know my heart; test me and know my anxious thoughts. See if there is any offensive way in me, and lead me in the way everlasting."

• Are you hesitant to pray these verses for yourself? Why? Where is that fear coming from?

_____

_____

_____

_____

• Confess your fears to the Lord, and ask Him to help you believe that He loves you and has already paid for whatever the Holy Spirit will reveal in your heart. Then pray these verses to your Father. Pay attention to His voice—He may answer your prayer as you complete the following questions.

_____

_____

_____

_____

144

2. When has your indicator light come on lately? Remember, your indicator light is your experience of strong, negative emotions. Use the four diagnostic questions from the lesson to identify the unprovable thoughts that led to those emotions and the ways in which you then behaved incongruently with who you really are.

_____

_____

_____

_____

3. Write out your most common unprovable tapes. Then, note exactly what makes those tapes unprovable. Are they predicting the future? Are they attempting to get inside someone else's head and assume their thoughts and feelings? Are they overgeneralizing? Now write out a new tape of provable thoughts to be played the next time you encounter a similar situation. One tape that is useful to play in any given situation is based on the truths of Romans 8:28 and 2 Peter 1:3: "He is in this, and He is in me."

_____

_____

_____

_____

4. Now that your heart has been exposed, how do you feel? Are you tempted to either try to fix yourself by playing the role of resolver or to be a victim and despair? Don't give in. Rest in the love of your Father and thank the Holy Spirit for giving you eyes to see.

_____

_____

_____

_____

Chapter 8

Resting in Your Treasure

Step 4: Rest

H ere we are at the final step: rest. Listen once again to the invitation Jesus extends to His children:

Are you tired? Worn out?
Burned out on religion? Come to me.
Get away with me and you'll recover your life.
I'll show you how to take a real rest.
Walk with me and work with me—
watch how I do it.
Learn the unforced rhythms of grace.
I won't lay anything heavy or ill-fitting on you.
Keep company with me
and you'll learn to live freely and lightly.

—Matthew 11:28–30 The Message

In stark contrast to the orphan mentality we so often take on, this passage is a beautiful picture of belief, which leads to real rest. Throughout the pages of this book, we have walked through the steps toward rest that Jesus described as recorded in Matthew 11.

In the Gospel of Luke, Jesus contrasts two different approaches to rest. He describes the first type using a parable:

The ground of a certain rich man

yielded an abundant harvest.

He thought to himself, "What shall I do?

I have no place to store my crops."

Then he said, "This is what I'll do.

I will tear down my barns and build bigger ones,

and there I will store my surplus grain.

And I'll say to myself,

'You have plenty of grain laid up for many years.

Take life easy; eat, drink and be merry.'"

—Luke 12:16–19

Doesn't that sound an awful lot like those ads for retirement communities? I used to think those places sounded kind of boring, but as I slowly inch toward that stage of life, they actually sound pretty good. I mean, are they saying I don't have to mow the lawn? Hmmm. Yeah, I've put in my time. Sign me up. I was meant for that kind of life. This attitude, in line with Jesus' description of the farmer, reflects the American dream, doesn't it? *"I've* put in the long hours; *I've* worked hard for what *I've* earned, so *I* get to decide what to do with it."

In the film *Shenandoah*, Jimmy Stewart's character Charlie Anderson prays, "Lord, we cleared this land. We plowed it, sowed it, and harvested. We cooked the harvest. It wouldn't be here, we wouldn't be eating it, if we hadn't done it all ourselves. We worked dog-bone hard for every crumb and morsel, but we thank you just the same anyway, Lord, for this food we are about to eat. Amen."

Charlie's arrogant prayer may appall us, yet it reminds me a tiny bit of myself. His words sound an awful lot like the way I respond when Jesus talks about generosity, and His admonishments infringe on my plans for my golden years. They're called "golden years" for a reason, are they not? They're our reward—our trophy—for decades of hard work. "I've worked hard for what I've earned—me, not you—so I'm going to enjoy it."

What does rest mean to you? What are you looking forward to resting in? I think many of us would say we are looking forward to resting in our surplus. The farmer had a surplus, and he got lost in it. He got lost in the small picture he had worked for. This was God's response to him:

"You fool! This very night
your life will be demanded from you.
Then who will get what
you have prepared for yourself?"
This is how it will be with
whoever stores up things for themselves
but is not rich toward God.

—vv. 20–21

The same could be said of us. We end up as fools when we achieve aspects of our picture and then find ourselves resting in them because it is never truly rest. Even when you and the people you love are smack dab in the middle of your picture and are soaking up the satisfaction of life as you feel it should be, you know your enjoyment is only temporary. You know it is not going to last.

Have you ever experienced post-vacation depression? Have you ever gotten depressed before the vacation was even over because you knew it was going to end? Then you know exactly what I'm talking about. If our greatest joy lies in the attainment of our picture, then the anxiety never leaves, because even as we possess that which we desire, we know it can be taken from us at any moment. We are constantly trying to figure out how to stay there as long as we can.

If this life is all there is, then the farmer is right. We should eat, drink, and be merry, because there is nothing else. Why not live it up? But that is not true rest. We are called to more.

Consider Jesus' second picture of rest in Luke 12, the only kind of rest that is truly satisfying:

Then Jesus said to his disciples:
"Therefore I tell you, do not worry about your life,
what you will eat;
or about your body, what you will wear.
For life is more than food,
and the body more than clothes. . . .
And do not set your heart on
what you will eat or drink; do not worry about it.

For the pagan world runs after all such things,

and your Father knows that you need them.

But seek his kingdom, and these things

will be given to you as well."

—vv. 22–23; 29–31

Do you hear Jesus' charge to us in this passage? Seek His kingdom. We were designed and called to seek not the picture—even though it is a present, felt reality—but His kingdom. By seeking His kingdom, we rest, because we are doing what we were made to do. Walking in our true calling is life giving, not life-draining. We are actually more motivated and energized than ever before. Resting in Jesus does not promote laziness, it leads to vitality.

In his book, *My Utmost for His Highest*, Oswald Chambers paraphrased Jesus' offer of rest in this way:

> *"I will give you rest"– that is, "I will sustain you, causing you to stand firm." He is not saying, "I will put you to bed, hold your hand, and sing you to sleep." But, in essence, He is saying, "I will get you out of bed–out of your listlessness and exhaustion, and out of your condition of being half dead while you are still alive. I will penetrate you with the spirit of life, and you will be sustained by the perfection of vital activity."*

Because of Christ's sacrifice on our behalf, we no longer have to scrap and save to try to attain a fleeting picture. We don't have to worry, fret, and invest all our energies in things that won't last. As

"I don't want to trust You; I want to understand You. And since I can't understand You, then maybe You're not worth trusting after all."

we walk in our true identity as children of the King, remembering that our righteousness is secure and our provision is guaranteed, then we are free to turn our attention to the bigger picture, our true calling. It is almost as if we have been placed back into the Garden of Eden—not because life is perfect but because the gospel has given us all we require. Through His Son, God says, "I have provided everything you need. Now go and do what you were created to do as you rest in what I've already done."

Rest in the Provider, Not the Provision

It is crucial to distinguish between the provision and the Provider. Making this distinction will transform your relationships. Your spouse is at times the provision God uses to minister to you, but they are never the Provider. Neither is your job. Neither is your community. Neither are your friendships. We get mixed up sometimes, and we need to trace the provision back to the Provider. Then, with eyes on Him, we can thank Him for His provision but not be dependent upon His provision to the exclusion of worship of Him as the Provider.

Not only is God our faithful Provider who gives us what we need, He also delights in doing so. Jesus says, "Do not be afraid, little flock, for your Father has been pleased to give you the kingdom" (Luke 12:32).

Holding tightly to this truth in the brokenness of life is hard. I struggle with this tension daily. In my job, I hear a lot of horrible stories, and sometimes I get pretty disillusioned with God. My client might share about how she suffered terrible abuse, and

I will say to her in my mind, "Please don't say that. Please. I know where this is going." And then I'll say to God, "You look really bad here. Do you realize that? I don't know how I am going to explain You to her in such a way where You will come off looking good. How in the world am I going to convince her that you delight in giving her *good things* when she has

No person or circumstance can ever prevent you from doing what you were truly called to do.

suffered this horribly?" I say these things to God because I think I'm His PR rep. Have you ever felt that way? Have you ever prayed something like, "God, I am Your representative, so what kind of spin am I going to put on the deep pain my friend is experiencing so she doesn't walk away from You completely?"

I have an undergraduate degree in marketing, and I'm telling you, sometimes it's a lot easier to sell cereal than it is to sell Jesus.

I daily hear and experience what seem like discrepancies between God's character and the suffering of His children, and I want to say to Him, "I don't want to trust You; I want to understand You. And since I can't understand You, then maybe You're not worth trusting after all." There are days when I just want to go home and Netflix the pain away. I don't want to feel others' pain. I don't want to feel my own pain. I just want to escape the mess. I want to launch my children into the world and only communicate with them through social media. I want to retire and buy a golf cart and make life all about getting that peace and enjoyment I have worked for all these years. I want to live in a retirement community with all those people on the billboards who look like they are actually enjoying their lives because that is what life is meant for—not the mess around me. The people on the billboards aren't broken and hurting. It would be much easier to be around them, right?

If I believe those things, I am a fool.

You and I, we were not created for a life of self-indulgent leisure. We were created to reflect the glory of God and to bring His kingdom to bear in this broken world. This is the bigger picture, and because of who we are in Christ, we are free to rest in it. Luke 12 goes on:

Sell your possessions and give to the poor.
Provide purses for yourselves
that will not wear out,
a treasure in heaven that will never fail,
where no thief comes near and no moth destroys.
For where your treasure is,
there your heart will be also.

—vv. 33–34

One mark of maturity in Christ is that you are caught up in the bigger picture, the bigger questions. You say, "I may not understand, and this circumstance may not be in my picture, but You are in this. What is my role in what You are doing in this place in my life? How do I build Your kingdom in this particular situation that is breaking my heart, in this relationship with this loved one who will not get into my picture? How do I build Your kingdom in the midst of this pain?"

This calling is what you were made for. You were made to push back the darkness and shine a much-needed light (Matthew 5:16) in a world that is stumbling about in the pitch black, grasping at the here and now because they either do not know or cannot see their Creator. Don't lose your focus; don't get distracted by the smaller picture. Don't get lost. No person or circumstance can ever prevent you from doing what you were truly called to do. Each moment in your life—in the picture or out of the picture, broken or beautiful—holds the opportunity to live out your deepest desire to glorify God in a way that only you, His unique creation, can.

Don't forget the greater gospel story. It goes something like this:

There once was a King, a great, powerful, perfect King who had every single resource at His fingertips. His subjects were not just His subjects; they were His children. He loved them so much He said, "All I have is yours! Take it. Enjoy it. I created it for you." He gave them complete access to His throne room, and He loved nothing more than to sit with them and spend time with them, listening to their hearts, and teaching them His ways. When they chose to doubt His goodness and worship not Him but the things He had given them, His heart broke over their doubt; He wept for what followed their disbelief—insecurity, discontentment, and fear.

He said, "I have a plan," and He told His Son beside Him, "It's time." The Son took off His robe and His crown; He laid down His scepter, put on the clothes of a commoner, and walked out the castle gates. To be among them. To be one of them. He served them and loved them. He spoke of the goodness of the King. He then laid down His very life so they could be rescued from the darkness of their hearts that they just couldn't shake. It was the only way.

Imagine the people's surprise when the Son appeared at His Father's side once again, victorious and whole. The King declared again to His people, "Everything I have is yours—not just My creation but My strength, My power, My wisdom, and My presence. When you're tempted to doubt that what I've given you is enough, when you're hurt and confused, come to Me. Let Me remind you again of what I have given you, of what I have done for you because I love you (Romans 8:32). And when you gaze a little too long at My creation, take matters into your own hands, and run away, come back. Sit with Me. Don't hide your face; look Me in the eyes. You'll find forgiveness and compassion there (1 John 1:9). Let Me remind you of My love for you, of My desires for you that are greater than anything you could desire for yourself (Ephesians 3:20). Let Me remind you of your name. Let Me energize you once again with a vision for the kingdom that goes far beyond what you can see. Let Me remind you of the role you play in that vision. Let Me show you once again the resources I have given you to carry out that role (2 Peter 1:3). They are endless, and they are yours."

The subjects didn't always heed the king's invitation. But when they did, they experienced a renewal of purpose and energy, powered by the love of their good King. They said, "Of course. I remember now! This is what I was created to do! This is who I was created to be!" And they rested in sweet relationship with the King.

Dearly loved child of the King, don't forget the story. Don't get lost in the smaller picture. You are taken care of, and you are free. Your Father wants you right by His side, plowing the field of life together, building His kingdom—the greater picture—for His glory and your good. Ask Him to disturb you out of your appetite for unstable, fleeting fulfillment and make you hungry for His offer of eternal, life-giving purpose. You have everything you need.

Rest.

Process Questions

1. Review the Exposure of a Gap chart from chapter 3. Which step toward rest do you feel is hardest for you? Why?

_____

_____

_____

_____

2. Read Luke 12:16–19. How do you see yourself attempting, like the farmer, to rest in the earthly treasure of what you think you've earned and deserve? Why does this approach never result in real rest?

_____

_____

_____

_____

3. What are some ways in which you have looked to God's provision to give you what only the Provider can give?

_____

_____

_____

_____

4. Describe the rest offered in Jesus. How do you feel when you consider this kind of rest that requires your complete trust and vulnerability? Relieved? Anxious?

_____

_____

_____

_____

5. What is God calling you to, beyond your picture? Remember, He has given you everything you need to glorify Him, no matter the circumstance.

_____

_____

_____

_____

IF YOU ENJOYED THIS BOOK, WILL YOU CONSIDER SHARING THE MESSAGE WITH OTHERS?

Let us know your thoughts at info@newhopepublishers.com. You can also let the author know by visiting or sharing a photo of the cover on our social media pages or leaving a review at a retailer's site. All of it helps us get the message out!

Twitter.com/NewHopeBooks
Facebook.com/NewHopePublishers
Instagram.com/NewHopePublishers

———————

New Hope® Publishers is a division of
Iron Stream Media, which derives its name from
Proverbs 27:17, "As iron sharpens iron,
so one person sharpens another."

This sharpening describes the process of discipleship, one to another. With this in mind, Iron Stream Media provides a variety of solutions for churches, missionaries, and nonprofits ranging from in-depth Bible study curriculum and Christian book publishing to custom publishing and consultative services. Through the popular Life Bible Study and Student Life Bible Study brands, ISM provides web-based full-year and short-term Bible study teaching plans as well as printed devotionals, Bibles, and discipleship curriculum.

For more information on ISM and New Hope Publishers, please visit
IronStreamMedia.com
NewHopePublishers.com